I0767159

Preface

In today's world of lightning-fast information sharing, it's become more important than ever to be able to distinguish truth from the overwhelming noise. "Silent Echoes" is a journey that sheds light on the subtle forces that shape public opinion, influence personal decisions, and impact society as a whole. As we delve into this enlightening compendium, you'll be challenged in a gentle yet firm way.

The narrative may push you out of your comfort zone, urging you to re-examine the values and beliefs that you've held for a long time. It's important to approach each chapter and insight with an open mind, free from prejudice and preconceptions. An open mind is the key to unlocking the secrets of understanding and awareness. It doesn't mean you're giving up your intellectual rigour, but rather that you're committed to engaging with the material sincerely and thoughtfully. So join us on this journey, and let's discover the hidden forces that shape our lives.

To truly absorb the intricate nuances and wisdom within the chapters of "Silent Echoes," one must approach it with a curious mind. While reading, you may come across beliefs and convictions that you've held for a long time, which might now gleam under the scrutiny and analysis of the book. Rather than being defensive, be fascinated by these moments. The objective here is not to tear down your intellectual structure but to ensure it has a solid foundation that is authentic and entirely your own.

"Silent Echoes" is a call for intellectual autonomy, a guide that will help you navigate the constant signals, cues, and messages that try to capture your attention and allegiance. This book is not only a tool for understanding but also for empowerment. It provides strategies to free your consciousness from the invisible chains that subtly bind it.

By engaging with this text, you will take a step towards personal liberation and a societal renaissance. You will learn how to recognize, understand, and master the "Silent Echoes". This reading adventure is not just about gaining knowledge but also about reclaiming your intellectual sovereignty and shaping the future.

So, dive into this book with a hunger for the truth. Within its pages, you will find the power to transform yourself and the world around you.

Embark on a transformative voyage of exploration, enlightenment, and empowerment. Join us on a journey of self-discovery through "Silent Echoes".

Silent Echoes

Illuminating the Covert Forces
of Influence

Aldo Grech

Table of Contents:

Echoes of Disenchantment

In the heart of a bustling city, the sun began its descent, painting the sky with strokes of orange and pink. At a small café, nestled under the protective branches of an ancient oak tree, sat Alex and Jordan, their coffee casting steamy silhouettes into the cool air. The world around them buzzed with life, but they were absorbed in a world of their own, a world woven with words of concern and contemplation.

Jordan stared into the swirling depths of his cup, his brow furrowed. "You know, Alex," he began, his voice heavy with thought, "I've been pondering over a question that seems to echo in the silent spaces of our society: 'What has democracy done for me?' It's a haunting refrain, growing louder with each passing day."

Alex leaned back, eyes fixed on the fading light. "It's a sign of our times," she murmured. "We're witnessing an alarming trend where the disenfranchised question
the very fabric of our democracy. It's as if the memory of world conflicts and the sacrifices for freedom have dimmed in our collective consciousness."

The conversation flowed as the city lights began to twinkle to life. They spoke of the growing chasm of economic inequality, the shadow that cast a long, dark silhouette over the ideals of democracy. Jordan's voice grew tense as he described the frustration and disillusionment breeding in the hearts of those who felt left behind.

Alex picked up the thread, her words painting a picture of a society fragmented by political polarization, a place where extreme ideologies took root in the fertile soil of discontent. "And let's not forget the erosion of trust," she added, her gaze turning towards the bustling street, "in our institutions, our media, our very governance. It's leading to a dangerous cynicism about the efficacy of democracy itself."

As the evening wore on, their conversation delved deeper into the issues plaguing their world. They spoke of AI, climate change, racial inequality, and economic insecurity—wounds that democracy seemed incapable of healing. With each word, the weight of their responsibility, their role in this unfolding narrative, grew heavier.

"But what's the path forward?" Jordan asked a note of desperation in his voice. "With authoritarianism's shadow looming large, how do we convince others, and perhaps even ourselves, that the alternative is not a leap into freedom but a fall into darkness?"

Alex's response was measured, a counterpoint to the rising tide of despair. "We look to history," she said firmly, "to the lessons taught by the rise and fall of authoritarian regimes. We make the case for democracy, not as a perfect system, but as our best hope for upholding the values of freedom, equality, and the rule of law."

They talked about engaging with the disillusioned, of acknowledging the legitimacy of their frustrations while advocating for active participation in the democratic process. As the night settled in, the café became a beacon of light, a small but defiant stand against the encroaching darkness.

As they stood to leave, the conversation lingered in the air, a silent echo of their resolve. "It's a daunting task," Jordan said, a hint of determination in his voice.

Alex nodded, "But one worth undertaking. For the sake of democracy, for our future."

They stepped out into the night, two figures against the vast tapestry of the city, their resolve as steadfast as the ancient oak that sheltered them.

As Alex and Jordan stepped onto the dimly lit streets, the city's pulse seemed to resonate with their deepening conversation. The night air was cool, a gentle contrast to the warmth of their debate.

Jordan broke the silence, his voice tinged with a new layer of complexity. "But Alex, what about those who don't see the rise of authoritarianism as a threat? Those who believe these alternatives are just different paths, not the cliff edge we perceive them to be?"

Alex paused, considering the question. "It's a challenging perspective," she admitted. "Many see the establishment as the real authoritarian force, labelling any threat to it as a false alarm. They view our concerns as fearmongering."

They walked in thoughtful silence, their footsteps echoing off of the buildings. "It's a narrative that's gaining traction," Jordan added, his words floating in the cool night air. "Some believe that what we call authoritarianism is simply a break from traditional politics, a challenge to the status quo."

Alex nodded slowly. "That's the heart of the problem, isn't it? This perception that what's different must be better, or at least worth trying. It's a seductive idea, especially for those who feel marginalized by the current system."

They reached a quiet park, the city's skyline a distant backdrop. Sitting on a bench beneath a canopy of stars, they continued their discourse.

"But how do we address this, Alex?" Jordan asked, his gaze fixed on the night sky. "How do we argue for democracy when it's seen as the very symbol of oppression by some?"

Alex leaned forward, her eyes reflecting the earnestness of her thoughts. "We need to reframe the narrative. It's not about defending an imperfect system blindly. It's about recognizing the fundamental rights and freedoms that democracy strives to protect, rights that are often the first casualties under authoritarian rule."

Jordan's expression was pensive. "So, it's about painting a bigger picture? Showing that while democracy isn't flawless, it's a system that allows for change, for voices to be heard?"

"Exactly," Alex replied. "We need to highlight the examples where democracy has adapted and evolved. We have to show that the alternative (authoritarianism), isn't just a different path, but one that historically leads to less freedom, less opportunity for change."

They delved into historical examples, discussing regimes where the allure of a strong, decisive leader led to the erosion of personal liberties and justice. They talked about how fear and division were often tools used to consolidate power, leading to societies where dissent was dangerous.

"But what if this doesn't convince them?" Jordan wondered aloud. "What if the allure of a 'strong' alternative continues to blind people to the risks?"

Alex sighed a mixture of resolve and realism in his voice. "Then we keep the dialogue open. We can't force people to see the world as we do, but we can present the facts, share our perspectives, and hope to spark a flame of understanding. Democracy is about that ongoing conversation, that continuous struggle for a better system."

As the night deepened, their conversation became a microcosm of the larger debate unfolding in societies around the world. The challenge was daunting, but as they rose from the bench and headed back into the city, their resolve was clear.

In a world teetering on the edge of profound change, their voices, though seemingly silent in the grand chorus of society, echoed with the timeless struggle for democracy and freedom. The chapter of their conversation might have ended, but the story, their relentless pursuit of understanding and advocacy for democracy, was just beginning.

Introduction

This book casts a discerning eye towards the elite colloquially and collectively called the 1%. It is crucial at the outset to clarify that the critique presented in these pages is not born out of disdain or envy towards this group. I've engaged with and even admired, several individuals within this elite echelon. These are individuals whose acumen, determination, and, in many cases, relentless pursuit of their passions have propelled them into the spheres of affluence and influence.

However, it is imperative to understand that the 1% is not a monolithic entity. It encompasses individuals who've perhaps unscrupulously amassed wealth, as well as those who have navigated their way to the top through genuine, well-intentioned endeavours. What warrants scrutiny and critique is not their success per se but the societal and cultural lenses through which we evaluate and celebrate success.

Our culture has, over time, narrowly defined 'success', lionizing wealth accumulation as its primary, if not sole, indicator. This book posits that success is a multifaceted phenomenon, warranting a more nuanced understanding and acknowledgment. There are myriad ways individuals contribute to and thrive within society, and these alternative narratives of success are deserving of celebration and respect, an aspect often overshadowed by the glaring spotlight on the affluent.

Moreover, the responsibility accompanying wealth is a focal point of this discourse. Wealth, particularly when it is accrued through the contributions and labour of the broader populace, the 99%, should be equitably redistributed. Taxation is a primary mechanism for this redistribution, ensuring that the elite contribute their fair share to the societal pot. Philanthropy, while commendable, is not a substitute for this fiscal responsibility. Often, the funds allocated to charitable endeavours are dwarfed by the sums saved through tax avoidance strategies, with philanthropy sometimes serving as a veneer for conscience appeasement or image cultivation, rather than a genuine commitment to societal betterment.

Furthermore, there is a pressing need for 'make-good' contributions, particularly from industries that exact a toll on the environment and society. These contributions are not penalties but responsibilities, ensuring that corporate activities' environmental degradation and societal impact are mitigated and rectified.

"Silent Echoes" delves into the covert strategies employed by some within the 1% to influence public opinion and sway political landscapes subtly. Through the dissemination of subliminal messages, promotion of conspiracy theories, and other insidious tactics, segments of the population are nudged, often unknowingly, to support political entities and parties that, paradoxically, work against their interests. These politicians and parties backed and financed by the elite, often enact policies that further consolidate wealth and power within the top tier, perpetuating a cycle of inequality and disempowerment. The pages ahead unfold this intricate tapestry, illuminating the "Silent Echoes" reverberating through our societal canyons, influencing minds and shaping narratives in ways more profound and pervasive than we might realise.

Please Note:
While this book may appear to adopt a predominantly U.S.-centric perspective, it is essential to clarify that I am not an American, and this approach is not intentional. The immense global influence wielded by the United States cannot be ignored,

given its significant impact on international affairs and economies. There's a saying in Australia that aptly encapsulates this dynamic: "When the U.S. sneezes, the rest of the world catches a cold." This phrase succinctly illustrates the ripple effects of America's actions and decisions across the globe. Consequently, although the text may seem steeped in "Americanism," it is crucial for you to recognize that no corner of the world is entirely insulated from the substantial shifts and events occurring within the United States. Hence, the issues discussed, while illustrated through an American lens, bear relevance and implications for people and societies worldwide.

For those in countries that have not yet encountered the extremes highlighted in these US-centric examples, this book should serve as a cautionary tale. It illustrates the potential consequences that could arise if we do not remain vigilant regarding the issues discussed.

From Customers and Employees to Shareholders

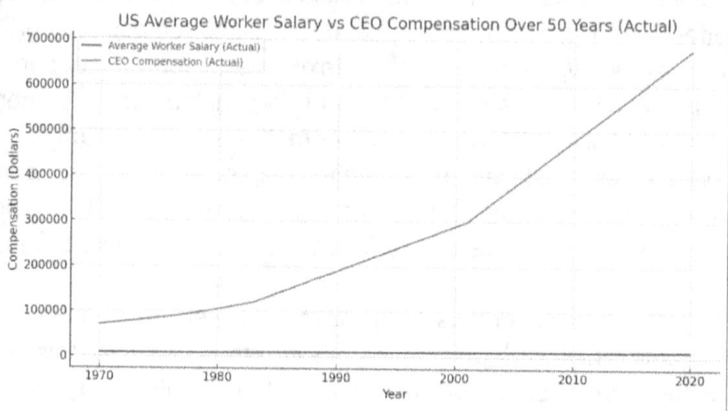

The trend in actual average US worker salaries compared to CEO compensation over the last 50 years indicates that while the average worker salary has experienced a gradual and marginal increase, CEO compensation has risen at a much more significant rate.

The disparity between the growth in worker salaries and CEO compensation becomes increasingly pronounced from the late 20th century onwards. This disparity highlights the expanding income gap, where the compensation of top executives has escalated at a far greater pace than the average worker's. The steep rise in CEO compensation, especially noticeable in the latter half of the graph, underscores the growing economic inequality within the corporate sector.

The average worker salary in the EU has seen a steady, gradual increase, reflecting a consistent growth over time. This growth is indicative of economic development and possibly the impact of labour laws and social welfare policies commonly found in European countries.

On the other hand, the rate of increase in CEO compensation is higher than that of the average worker, but it does not show the exponential growth often seen in the United States. This trend may be attributed to different corporate governance practices, cultural attitudes towards executive remuneration, and a more regulated business environment in Europe.

While there has been an upward trend in compensation for both workers and CEOs in Europe, the gap between the two is less pronounced compared to trends observed in the US. This reflects the more balanced approach to income distribution and executive compensation prevalent in European economic systems.

The widening chasm between CEO salaries and the minimum wage serves as an emblematic symbol of shifting priorities within the business world. This stark income inequality (magnified in the US), transcends mere economic concerns; it represents a profound reflection of the values that guide our society. To confront these pressing challenges, an urgent call for recalibration echoes through the corridors of corporate decision-making. This recalibration underscores the imperative of reevaluating and redefining the values that underpin our economic systems. It beckons us to prioritize the well-being of all stakeholders; customers, employees, and shareholders alike; in our collective pursuit of a more equitable and just economy. It is a rallying cry for a renewed commitment to shared prosperity and an unwavering resolve to address the persistent income inequality that continues to cast a shadow over our society.

The surge in CEO salaries over the past several decades is a striking testament to the changing landscape of corporate compensation. This meteoric rise commenced in the 1970s when CEOs earned approximately 20 times the average salary of a typical worker. However, this relatively modest pay gap between executives and employees soon gave way to an era of extravagant executive compensation. By the early 21st century, this ratio had ballooned to almost 300 times the earnings of the average worker. To understand this dramatic transformation, we must delve into the underlying factors that fueled it.

One pivotal driver of the exponential growth in CEO salaries was the introduction of stock options and performance-based bonuses within executive compensation packages. These innovative incentives dramatically altered the landscape of corporate remuneration by tying CEO pay directly to short-term gains in stock prices. Consequently, CEOs were increasingly compelled to prioritize the interests of shareholders above all else. In their pursuit of boosting their companies' stock performance, CEOs often resorted to implementing cost-cutting measures, which frequently came at the expense of the workforce. This shift in executive incentives and priorities laid the foundation for the yawning income inequality that characterizes our present-day economic landscape.

The introduction of stock options and performance-based bonuses reshaped the compensation landscape by instituting a new paradigm emphasising short-term financial gains. This departure from traditional compensation models, which were anchored in base salaries, meant that CEOs had a personal stake in the company's stock price performance. Consequently, their primary focus shifted from the long-term health and stability of the organization to delivering immediate returns to shareholders.

This realignment of incentives resulted in a corporate culture that often prioritized cost-cutting measures to maximize profitability and appease investors. Layoffs, reductions in employee benefits, and outsourcing became common strategies for trimming expenses, all of which had direct consequences for the workforce. Workers found themselves bearing the brunt of these cost-cutting initiatives as they experienced stagnant wages, diminished job security, and an erosion of labour rights.

The shift in CEO compensation structures and the ensuing focus on delivering short-term gains for shareholders have redefined corporate priorities. While corporate leaders were once tasked with stewarding their organizations' long-term growth and fostering a sense of responsibility towards employees and communities, the predominant objective has been enhancing shareholder value.

This shareholder-centric approach often comes at the expense of other stakeholders, such as employees, customers, and society at large. The relentless pursuit of profitability has led to a "shareholder primacy" model, where the interests of investors reign supreme. This corporate ethos sometimes translates into decisions that prioritize cost-cutting measures, offshoring jobs, and reducing employee benefits, all of which contribute to income inequality and the erosion of workers' rights.

As confirmed by some Elites (see next chapter), the implications of the widening gap between CEO salaries and worker compensation extend beyond the corporate sphere. They reverberate throughout society, affecting economic stability, social cohesion, and the well-being of individuals and families. Income inequality fosters feelings of injustice and resentment among workers, potentially fueling social unrest and divisions.

Furthermore, the concentration of wealth in the hands of a few elite executives exacerbates cycles of poverty and hampers social mobility. The stagnant wages of low and middle-income workers make it increasingly challenging for them to access quality education, healthcare, and other essential services, perpetuating disparities across generations.

The inability of the minimum wage to keep pace with inflation and the cost of living has had profound implications for the economic well-being of individuals and families around the globe. While CEOs and corporate leaders have reaped the benefits of substantial salary increases, minimum-wage workers continue to grapple with the challenge of making ends meet on meagre earnings. This disconnect between the highest and lowest earners within organizations has underscored the need for a reevaluation of wage policies and a renewed commitment to addressing income inequality.

Furthermore, and less talked about is the tax system that favours the ultra-wealthy and corporations. Over the past half-century, the tax landscape in the United States has undergone significant changes, especially concerning the taxation of corporations and the ultra-wealthy, compared to the middle and working classes. This shift in tax policy reflects broader economic and political changes and has sparked ongoing debates about equity and fairness in the tax system.

In the early 1970s, corporate tax rates and the top marginal tax rates for individuals were substantially higher than they are today. The top corporate tax rate hovered around 48-52%, while the wealthiest individuals faced marginal tax rates of around 70%. These rates represented a progressive tax structure aimed at redistributing wealth and funding government initiatives.

However, since then, these rates have seen a marked decrease. The Tax Cuts and Jobs Act of 2017, for example, reduced the top corporate tax rate from 35% to 21%, while the top marginal tax rate for individuals dropped to 37%, significantly lower than the 70% rate of the early 1970s.

In recent years, there have been some similarities between the tax regimes in the US and Europe, with both regions making efforts to reduce taxes for multinational corporations and high-income earners.

However, the specific tax policies and outcomes can vary significantly across different countries in Europe, and the impact on different income groups can be complex.

In general, many European countries have implemented measures to reduce taxes on multinational corporations, such as lowering corporate tax rates and introducing special tax regimes for foreign investors.

This reduction in tax rates for corporations and the ultra-wealthy contrasts sharply with the tax burden on the middle and working classes. While the top earners have benefited from substantial tax cuts and loop-holes, the middle and lower income brackets have not seen equivalent relief. The middle class, in particular, often faces a relatively high tax burden when considering the combination of federal, state, and local taxes, along with payroll taxes. Unlike the ultra-wealthy, who can often leverage tax deductions, credits, and capital gains (which are taxed at lower rates), the middle and working classes usually derive their income from wages, which are taxed at standard rates without many of the benefits available to higher earners.

This divergence in tax treatment has led to criticisms of the current tax regime as being unjust and favouring the wealthy. Critics argue that the substantial tax cuts for the richest individuals and corporations have contributed to widening income inequality and reduced the government's ability to fund essential services and social programs. They point out that a more progressive tax system, similar to what existed in the 1970s, could help address these disparities by requiring those who have the most to contribute a larger share towards the collective needs of society.

The evolution of the tax system in the U.S. reflects deep-seated ideological differences about the role of government, the distribution of wealth, and the principles of fairness and equity in taxation. The debate continues to be a central issue in American politics, influencing policy decisions and shaping the economic landscape of the country.

Amidst the backdrop of escalating income inequality, a disconcerting phenomenon has taken root within corporate culture; the gaslighting effect. In an era where companies frequently emphasize their commitment to their workforce and customer satisfaction in their public narratives, a dissonance emerges when actions speak louder than words. The gap between what CEOs and corporate boards proclaim and the tangible outcomes for employees and customers, underscores a deeper issue.

This insidious gaslighting effect often unfolds in the form of corporate rhetoric that champions employee well-being and job security. Yet, beneath these proclamations lies a troubling reality; companies frequently resort to cost-cutting measures that result in workforce reductions and diminished benefits for employees. As executives articulate their unwavering dedication to employees, they simultaneously implement strategies that erode the very foundations of job security and economic stability.

The narrative perpetuated by CEOs and corporate leaders contends that prioritizing shareholders' interests ultimately serves the broader workforce. This argument posits that by maximizing profits and enhancing shareholder value, the long-term sustainability of the company is safeguarded, thereby preserving jobs. However, this narrative also known as trickle-down economics, conveniently sidesteps the stark truth that many workers find themselves grappling with ongoing economic hardships, while CEOs bask in the glow of substantial financial gains.

The gaslighting effect becomes particularly pronounced when contrasting the immense wealth accumulated by executives with the financial struggles experienced by a significant portion of the workforce. The divergence in outcomes is a stark reminder of the chasm that exists between the highest echelons of corporate leadership and the everyday employees who form the backbone of these organizations. This glaring disparity raises questions about the authenticity of corporate values and the true priorities that govern the modern corporate landscape.

In essence, the gaslighting effect within corporate culture underscores the need for a critical examination of the prevailing ethos within organizations. The disjunction between rhetoric and action calls for a reevaluation of corporate values and a commitment to fostering a more equitable distribution of the benefits derived from corporate success. Addressing this gaslighting phenomenon is not only essential for rectifying the systemic issues contributing to income inequality but also for restoring trust and accountability within the corporate world.

In essence, the societal implications of income inequality extend far beyond economic considerations. They touch upon the very essence of social cohesion and stability. Addressing this pressing issue necessitates not only a reevaluation of economic systems but also a commitment to fostering inclusivity, fairness, and equal opportunities for all members of society. By recognizing the far-reaching consequences of income inequality and actively working to rectify these disparities, we can aspire to build a more equitable and harmonious future for our communities.

Voices of Equity and Advocacy Among the Elite

In this chapter, we delve into the insights and impactful perspectives of a sample of the luminaries humanitarian billionaires and millionaires who have emerged as influential voices in the discourse on economic disparities. These individuals challenge the prevailing norms and advocate for a fundamental reassessment of economic principles, tax policies, and philanthropic endeavours. Their compelling messages underscore the necessity of cooperation, fair taxation, and a steadfast commitment to systemic change as essential components of genuine progress toward a more equitable society.

Through their impassioned advocacy, these figures exemplify how individuals of great wealth can transcend their own economic status to champion a vision of a world characterized by justice, fairness, and shared prosperity.

It's important to acknowledge that these individuals, like all humans, have their flaws and are not without imperfections. Paradoxically, it is precisely because of these imperfections that their views and words carry such tremendous weight and influence.

Abigail Disney, an American documentary filmmaker, philanthropist, and heiress to the Disney fortune, has been an outspoken advocate for addressing income inequality and wealth disparity. While she herself comes from a wealthy background, Abigail Disney has used her platform and resources to draw attention to the stark wealth divide in society. She is well-known for her critical views on excessive wealth accumulation and the need for the wealthy to pay higher taxes to address social and economic imbalances.

Disney's commitment to addressing income inequality is not just rhetoric; she has taken tangible actions to back up her beliefs. She made headlines by parting with a significant portion of her wealth, donating $72 million, and has consistently argued that the wealthy should bear a more substantial tax burden to support vital social programs and reduce inequality. Her stance gained further relevance during the COVID-19 pandemic, as the crisis exacerbated income disparities, making her calls for greater taxation on the rich even more pertinent.

Abigail Disney is part of an international coalition of wealthy individuals who share similar concerns about income inequality and advocate for higher taxes on the rich. Their collective message is clear; governments must take meaningful steps to address wealth inequality by implementing policies that require the wealthiest individuals to contribute more to society. Abigail Disney's dedication to using her privilege and resources to push for economic fairness highlights the potential for individuals from affluent backgrounds to become advocates for positive change in society.

Nick Hanauer, an entrepreneur who has achieved self-made billionaire status, is a prominent figure in contemporary discussions on income inequality and economic fairness. His background and beliefs offer a unique perspective that challenges conventional economic wisdom.

Hanauer's journey to wealth began with his entrepreneurial endeavours. He co-founded a startup called aQuantive, an online advertising company, in the 1990s. The company became a significant player in the digital marketing industry and was eventually acquired by Microsoft in 2007 for $6.4 billion. This achievement catapulted Hanauer into the ranks of billionaires, but it also gave him a platform to critically examine the economic system that had contributed to his success.

One of the central tenets of Hanauer's philosophy is his rejection of the prevailing notion that "greed is good." He contends that this ideology, which has long been championed by proponents of unregulated capitalism, is not only morally corrosive but also scientifically flawed. Hanauer's dissent stems from his belief that economics should be rooted in a more profound understanding of human behaviour and societal well-being.

In place of the "greed is good" mantra, Hanauer offers a new economic theory grounded in reciprocity and cooperation. He argues that a thriving economy should prioritize fair compensation for workers, promote sustainable business practices, and strive for equitable wealth distribution. Hanauer's vision challenges the conventional wisdom that the wealthy should prioritize their individual interests without considering the broader impact on society. He advocates for an economic paradigm that acknowledges the interdependence of all members of society and the role of cooperation in driving sustainable prosperity.

Nick Hanauer's perspective is characterized by his firsthand experience as an entrepreneur and a self-made billionaire. This unique vantage point allows him to critique the system from within, offering insights into the mechanisms that perpetuate income inequality. His advocacy for a more equitable and inclusive economic model has made him a prominent voice in the ongoing discourse on wealth disparity and social justice.

Warren Buffett, often referred to as the "Oracle of Omaha," stands as an iconic figure in the world of finance and investment. His remarkable career and insightful perspectives on income inequality have earned him a prominent place in the discourse on economic fairness.

Buffett's journey to becoming one of the wealthiest individuals on the planet is a testament to his exceptional acumen in investing. He began his investment career at a young age and eventually took control of Berkshire Hathaway, a textile company that would later transform into a conglomerate with diverse holdings, including major stakes in well-known companies like Coca-Cola, Apple, and American Express. Under his stewardship, Berkshire Hathaway evolved into a powerhouse in the world of finance and investment.

Beyond his professional achievements, Warren Buffett is renowned for his commitment to addressing income inequality through the concept known as the "Buffett Rule." This rule, which he has consistently advocated for, asserts that households earning over $1 million annually should not pay a lower percentage of their income in taxes than middle-class families. The crux of his argument lies in the stark reality that he, as a billionaire, pays a lower tax rate than his secretary, highlighting a significant flaw in the existing tax system.

Buffett's stance emphasizes the necessity of a fair and progressive tax system to bridge the wealth gap and ensure that the most affluent members of society contribute their equitable share to the collective good. His advocacy for a more just taxation system has made him a respected voice in the ongoing discussion about income inequality and the role of the super-wealthy in promoting economic fairness.

Warren Buffett's legacy extends far beyond his investment prowess; it encompasses his dedication to addressing the profound disparities in wealth and income that exist within society. His principled stance on tax reform and his willingness to use his influence to champion these issues continue to inspire conversations and action aimed at creating a more equitable economic landscape.

Rutger Bregman, a prominent historian and writer, gained international recognition for his bold and impassioned stance on addressing wealth inequality, particularly through the lens of taxation. His outspoken advocacy has made him a formidable voice in the ongoing dialogue surrounding economic fairness and the responsibilities of the world's wealthiest individuals and corporations.

Bregman's academic background in history informs his perspective on income inequality and its historical context. As a historian, he delves into the roots and evolution of societal structures and systems that have led to the current wealth disparities. This academic foundation provides him with a deep understanding of the historical forces at play in the ongoing debate about economic equity.

In 2019, Rutger Bregman made headlines during his appearance at the Davos World Economic Forum, a gathering of some of the world's most influential and affluent figures. His message was clear and unapologetic; it was time for billionaires and corporations to pay their fair share of taxes. He boldly critiqued what he termed "stupid philanthropy schemes," asserting that the primary issue demanding attention was tax avoidance. Bregman's comments struck a chord in a forum where discussions often revolved around charitable efforts rather than tackling the root causes of income inequality.

Bregman's analogy of a firefighters' conference where nobody discusses water succinctly encapsulated the urgency he felt in addressing tax avoidance as a fundamental solution to bridge the wealth divide. His approach disrupts the conventional narratives that often dominate discussions about wealth and philanthropy, pushing for a more direct and systemic approach to income inequality. This advocacy has catapulted him to the forefront of the conversation on equitable taxation and the role of the elite in shaping a more just economic landscape.

Bill Gates, a towering figure in the tech industry and one of the world's wealthiest individuals, has been a vocal advocate for addressing income inequality. His resume is a testament to his extraordinary success, as he co-founded Microsoft, the software giant that revolutionized personal computing. Gates played a pivotal role in shaping the modern technology landscape and accumulating substantial wealth in the process. However, rather than turning a blind eye to the growing wealth gap, Gates has dedicated himself to finding solutions.

One of Gates' notable beliefs centers around estate taxation. In a conversation with Forbes' Randall Lane, Gates expressed his view that the current estate tax rates should be even higher. This perspective is grounded in the recognition that extreme wealth concentration among a select few can perpetuate inequality across generations. Gates understands that a robust estate tax can help redistribute wealth and prevent the formation of dynastic fortunes that perpetuate privilege. His advocacy for this policy reflects his commitment to using his influence and resources to address the systemic issues contributing to income inequality.

Gates' charitable foundation, the Bill and Melinda Gates Foundation, is another testament to his commitment to tackling societal challenges. The foundation focuses on issues such as global health, poverty alleviation, and education. It has contributed significant funds to initiatives that aim to improve healthcare in underserved communities, eradicate diseases, and enhance educational opportunities worldwide. Gates recognizes that private philanthropy, while valuable, cannot substitute for systemic change and equitable taxation. His actions underscore his belief in the importance of combining charitable efforts with structural reforms to bridge the wealth gap and promote a fairer society.

The tangible outcomes from the actions of prominent figures like Abigail Disney, Nick Hanauer, Warren Buffett, Rutger Bregman, and Bill Gates in addressing economic disparities and advocating for tax reform are more nuanced and complex than straightforward legislative changes. These individuals, through their advocacy and public discourse, have significantly contributed to shaping the conversation around wealth inequality and fair taxation.

Warren Buffett's advocacy for higher taxes on the wealthy, encapsulated in the "Buffett Rule," did inspire some political action. The Obama administration proposed a tax plan in 2011 named after Buffett, aimed at ensuring that millionaires pay at least the same tax rate as middle-class Americans. However, this specific proposal faced legislative challenges and was not enacted as law.

Abigail Disney's role as an outspoken critic of wealth accumulation and her advocacy for higher taxes on the wealthy have been instrumental in bringing issues of income inequality into the public domain. While direct legislative outcomes linked to her advocacy are difficult to pinpoint, her efforts have undeniably contributed to a broader awareness and discussion of these critical issues.

Nick Hanauer's critiques of the "trickle-down" economic theory and his alternative views on wealth distribution and economic policy have influenced policymakers and the public alike. Although specific policy changes directly attributed to his advocacy are challenging to identify, his perspectives have certainly played a role in reshaping how economic policy is debated and understood.

Rutger Bregman gained international recognition for his bold stance at the Davos World Economic Forum, where he called for effective tax reforms to address wealth inequality. While direct policy changes resulting from his statements are hard to trace, his blunt critique of tax avoidance by the wealthy added significant momentum to the global conversation on fair taxation and economic equity.

Bill Gates, through his advocacy for higher estate taxes and his philanthropic work in global health and education, demonstrates the potential impact of affluent individuals in addressing systemic societal issues. The influence of the Bill and Melinda Gates Foundation in areas like the eradication of diseases and improvement of healthcare infrastructure in developing countries is a testament to Gates' commitment. However, directly linking his advocacy to specific tax policies in individual countries is less clear.

In essence, the actions of these individuals highlight the role that advocacy and public discourse can play in influencing public opinion and shaping the environment for potential policy changes, even if direct legislative outcomes are not immediately apparent. Their contributions to the dialogue on wealth disparity and social justice continue to inspire conversations and actions aimed at creating a more equitable economic landscape.

In light of the profound insights and actions of these influential figures, it becomes our collective responsibility to carry forward this momentum. By amplifying their voices, we can extend their message to every corner of society, galvanizing a widespread movement that calls for equitable taxation and economic justice. It's crucial that we unite in our efforts to exert pressure on the wealthiest 1% and their political allies, urging them to respond to our collective demand for a fairer tax system. This united front is essential in shaping a future where economic fairness isn't just an ideal, but a reality.

Echoes of Privilege

In the intricate tapestry of modern politics, a pattern emerges, one that finds its roots in the turmoil and upheaval of the French Revolution. Corey Robin's analysis of the origins of the political right provides a compelling historical perspective on contemporary political dynamics. His thesis suggests that the political right, as we know it today, has its roots in the reaction to the French Revolution. This pivotal event significantly altered the social and political landscape of the time.

The French Revolution, which began in 1789, was a radical movement that upended the centuries-old feudal system in France. It was driven by ideals encapsulated in the famous motto "Liberté, égalité, fraternité" (Liberty, equality, fraternity). These ideals represented a seismic shift away from the feudal norms of hierarchy and privilege, advocating instead for a society based on democratic principles, equal rights, and the rule of law.

The aristocracy, which had long enjoyed privileged status under the Ancien Régime, found their very existence threatened by these revolutionary ideals. Their response to this threat was not merely defensive but took the form of an organized counter-movement. This reactionary stance was fundamentally about preserving their status, privileges, and traditional hierarchies that the revolution sought to dismantle.

Robin argues that this reaction by the aristocracy against the egalitarian principles of the French Revolution set the foundational ideology of what would become the political right. This ideology was characterized by a strong inclination towards preserving traditional social structures, a preference for hierarchical organization of society, and a scepticism, if not outright rejection, of egalitarian reforms.

Over the centuries, the issues and expressions of the political right have evolved. In different historical contexts, this has encompassed support for monarchies, opposition to socialist and communist movements, advocacy for free-market capitalism, and resistance to social welfare policies. In the contemporary era, it often manifests as support for free enterprise, scepticism of government intervention in the economy, and the championing of individual liberties, albeit with a tendency to preserve existing social hierarchies.

However, as Robin posits, underlying these changing issues is a consistent thread: a fundamental opposition to the radical redistribution of power and resources advocated by various egalitarian movements since the French Revolution. This includes resistance to policies that significantly alter the status quo of economic and social power structures, in favour of the 99%.

Robin's analysis suggests that understanding the modern political right requires looking at how historical reactions to revolutionary change have shaped and continue to influence contemporary political ideologies and debates. This perspective offers a lens through which to view current political divides, not just as contemporary phenomena but as part of a longer historical continuum influenced by the foundational events of the French Revolution.

This historical backdrop sets the stage for understanding a paradoxical phenomenon in contemporary politics: the support of right-wing parties by those they deem the "lesser class." Several factors contribute to this seemingly contradictory allegiance. Firstly, there's the innate human resistance to change. Many individuals, apprehensive about the uncertainties of transformative ideologies, find solace in the right's promise to preserve the status quo. This allure of stability often overrides the desire for progressive change.

Yet, there is an inherent paradox in the relationship between conservatism and the broader public, particularly those who may be apprehensive about change. Conservatism, as a political and social philosophy, often emphasizes the preservation of traditional institutions, values, and practices. It tends to advocate for stability, order, and continuity, resisting rapid or radical changes in society.

For many individuals, especially those who experience uncertainty or instability in their lives, the appeal of conservatism lies in its promise of stability and predictability. It offers a sense of security by upholding known structures and norms, as opposed to the unknowns that come with significant change. This can be particularly attractive in times of rapid social, economic, or technological transformations that might feel overwhelming or threatening to one's way of life.

However, this appeal to stability can paradoxically work against the interests of the masses who fear change. While conservatism might resist disruptive changes, it usually hinders progress and reforms that benefit the broader population. For instance, conservative policies oppose the redistribution of wealth, comprehensive healthcare reforms, or measures to address social inequality, under the guise of maintaining economic stability and traditional social structures. As a result, the very individuals who seek refuge in the stability promised by conservatism find themselves disadvantaged by the lack of progressive change in areas that improve their quality of life and economic well-being.

Moreover, the resistance to change inherent in conservative ideology often leads to a romanticization of the past and an idealization of historical social structures that were inherently unequal. This nostalgia overlooks the historical injustices and disparities that progress and change have sought to address.

Therefore, while conservatism might resonate with a public fear of change by offering a sense of stability and continuity, it can also maintain and reinforce existing social and economic disparities. For those who are already disadvantaged within these structures, conservatism's resistance to change can mean the perpetuation of their challenges, rather than their alleviation. Recognizing and navigating this paradox is a crucial aspect of political discourse and policy-making, especially in efforts to balance the need for stability with the imperative for social and economic progress.

Identity politics plays a significant role. Right-wing entities expertly weave narratives that tap into a collective identity based on ethnicity, religion, or cultural values. This strategy creates a sense of belonging and community among voters, who then view these parties as the guardians of their shared identity.

For the elite, conservatism serves as a means to preserve their status, power, and economic interests. Their advocacy for conservative policies and resistance to change is typically rooted in a desire to maintain the existing social and economic hierarchies that benefit them. This includes preserving favourable tax structures, regulatory environments, and other systems that uphold their privileged position. The elite's embrace of conservatism is thus often driven by self-interest and the preservation of their wealth and influence.

On the other hand, for many in the 99%, the appeal of conservatism can stem from a desire for stability and security in their lives. This demographic often fears rapid change not because they necessarily benefit from the status quo in the same way the elite do, but because change brings uncertainty. Their support for conservative policies may be based on the belief that these policies will maintain social order, protect traditional values, and provide a sense of continuity in a rapidly changing world. For them, conservatism can represent a safeguard against the disruptions and dislocations that can accompany dramatic societal shifts.

However, this perspective of the 99% can sometimes be at odds with their long-term interests. While conservative policies might offer a sense of immediate security and familiarity, they hinder the implementation of reforms that address systemic issues like economic inequality, healthcare accessibility, and educational opportunities. Thus, the conservatism supported by many within the 99% inadvertently contributes to the maintenance of a status quo that does not necessarily serve their best interests or the well-being of all.

This dichotomy reflects the complex dynamics of political ideologies and their appeal to different segments of society. It underscores the need for nuanced and empathetic political discourse that acknowledges the diverse motivations behind support for conservatism. It also highlights the importance of educating and engaging the broader public on how various policies impact their lives, not just in the short term but in the long-term context of societal progress and equity.

Populist rhetoric is a potent tool in the right's arsenal. They often position themselves as champions of the "common people," vowing to battle elites and uphold the interests of the average citizen. This rhetoric, though frequently laced with over-simplifications and false dichotomies, resonates with those who feel marginalized or unheard by the political establishment.

Economic anxiety cannot be overlooked. In times of financial instability, right-wing parties promise economic revival, job creation, and a return to prosperity. These promises, often lacking concrete plans or rooted in regressive policies, nonetheless appeal to those struggling in the current economic climate.

Finally, there's the widespread distrust of the political establishment. Disillusionment with traditional political players drives voters towards those who promise to disrupt the status quo. Right-wing parties often position themselves as the antithesis of the establishment, attracting those frustrated with the perceived inefficiencies and corruption of mainstream politics.

This understanding brings us to the subtle yet pervasive influence of gaslighting and meme culture in modern politics. The right, skilled in the art of narrative manipulation, uses these tools to shape public opinion and reinforce their ideologies. Gaslighting, a psychological tactic that makes individuals question their reality, is employed to cast doubt on progressive ideas and movements. Memes, in their simplicity and virality, become carriers of these distorted narratives, often laden with misinformation and appealing to emotional rather than rational responses.

The propagation of these memes by the very people they disenfranchise reveals the complexity of political manipulation. It underscores the effectiveness of the right's strategies in framing their agenda in a way that resonates with a broad swath of the populace, often against their own interests. These "echoes of privilege" reverberate through the political landscape, subtly shaping perceptions and choices, steering the narrative away from egalitarian ideals and towards the preservation of traditional power structures.

Beyond Polarization

In the contemporary landscape of public discourse, societal debates frequently devolve into a quagmire of semantics, often manipulated to serve the interests of those in power. Terms like left versus right, liberal against conservative, and progressive versus traditional become the lexicon of division, obscuring the real issues at play. This oversimplification of complex issues into binary oppositions is so deeply ingrained in our public conversations that it's easy to lose sight of the actual matters at stake. We are often left bewildered, grappling with the essence of what we are truly contending with.

Upon closer examination, it becomes evident that the genuine conflict transcends these superficial political dichotomies. What we are witnessing is a profound clash that cuts to the core of our collective ethos - a battle between empathy and discrimination, truth and lies, and the realm of science versus the allure of conspiracy theories.

The idea of viewing economic pursuits as a win/lose scenario contributes to a form of discrimination, reinforcing the flawed misconception that those who end up on the losing side somehow deserve poverty, while winners claim everything. In contrast, a more inclusive approach seeks mutually beneficial outcomes and emphasizes a fair distribution of wealth. At its core, this approach values empathy and extends care beyond the self. It's evident that the concept of scarcity is used as a tool of suppression by some of the 1%. In contrast, genuine wealth is found in the spirit of sharing and collective growth. The true essence of prosperity lies not in a winner-takes-all mentality but in fostering a sense of unity where everyone can thrive together, at the very heart of which lies empathy and care for others in addition to and beyond self

Empathy, as explored in the chapter, "The Distortion of Empathy", the capacity to understand and share the feelings of another, stands as a bulwark against discrimination, which is often rooted in fear, misunderstanding, and a refusal to acknowledge the shared threads of our humanity. In our current social and political climate, empathy is not just a personal virtue but a societal imperative, critical for addressing issues of inequality, injustice, and human rights.

Empathy is about understanding and sharing the feelings of others, which requires a level of emotional intelligence and compassion. It's about recognizing that our experiences and perspectives are not the only ones that matter and being willing to listen to and learn from others.

On the other hand, discrimination is a sign of weakness. It's rooted in fear, ignorance, and a lack of understanding of others. Discrimination means treating people differently based on factors like race, gender, sexuality, or religion, and it can lead to oppression, violence, and inequality.

While some people may argue that discrimination is a sign of strength or power, it's actually a reflection of insecurity and a lack of understanding. By embracing empathy and rejecting discrimination, we can build stronger and more inclusive communities, and create a more just and equitable world.

Moreover, the rise of digital media has both democratized access to information and created new challenges for sorting truth from falsehood. On one hand, the internet has made it possible for anyone with an internet connection to access a wealth of information and perspectives that were previously unavailable or inaccessible. On the other hand, the ease of publishing and sharing information has also made it possible for misinformation, disinformation, and propaganda to spread like wildfire.

This has had serious implications for democracy and governance, as misinformation can erode trust in democratic institutions, fuel polarization and extremism, and undermine the ability of citizens to make informed decisions. It has also had significant impacts on public health, as misinformation about vaccines, medical treatments, and health risks can lead to misinformed decisions and dangerous consequences.

Lastly, the dichotomy between science and conspiracy theories represents a clash between two fundamentally different ways of thinking and understanding the world. Science is built on a commitment to evidence, reason, and critical thinking. It relies on rigorous testing, peer review, and a willingness to update beliefs in the face of new evidence.

In contrast, conspiracy theories tend to be based on suspicion, speculation, and a distrust of authority and expertise. They often rely on cherry-picking or misinterpreting evidence, making logical fallacies, and appealing to emotional responses rather than reasoned arguments.

This conflict is not just about differences in opinion. It's about the tension between a commitment to evidence and a tendency towards conjecture and speculation.
It also highlights the importance of media literacy and critical thinking skills, as well as the need for a culture of trust and openness in science and public discourse more broadly.

In extending this exploration, it becomes apparent that these core conflicts—between empathy and discrimination, truth and lies, science and conspiracy—are not isolated phenomena. They are interconnected, each feeding into and influencing the others. For instance, the rejection of scientific understanding can fuel discrimination, while the spread of misinformation can erode empathy. Addressing these challenges, therefore, requires a holistic approach that recognizes these interdependencies.

Our collective task is to navigate these turbulent waters with a renewed commitment to empathy, a steadfast dedication to the truth, and an unwavering belief in the principles of scientific inquiry. It is only through this lens that we can hope to move beyond the semantic games that dominate our public discourse and address the real issues that define our times. This journey is not just about changing the conversation; it's about transforming the very foundations of how we engage with one another and the world around us.

At the heart of today's reimagined societal conflicts lies a profound struggle, one that surpasses the often superficial and divisive nature of politics. This struggle is not primarily about ideology or partisanship but rather centres on the human capacity for empathy and the pitfalls of discrimination. Empathy, the deeply ingrained ability to understand, share, and connect with the emotions and experiences of others, is not just a personal virtue; it is a societal cornerstone that transcends political boundaries and ideologies, delving into the very essence of human connection, compassion, and understanding.

In stark contrast to empathy stands discrimination – an all-too-common blight rooted in prejudice, ignorance, and often a willful disregard for the shared threads of our humanity. Discrimination is more than just an individual failing; it is a societal poison that erodes the fabric of communities, creating rifts and perpetuating injustices. It thrives in environments where empathy is lacking, where understanding and compassion are replaced with judgment and exclusion.

In the current social and political climate, issues such as social justice, equality, and human rights have come to the fore, often framed within political discourse. However, these are not merely topics for debate or political maneuvering; they are the battlegrounds where empathy confronts discrimination. These issues demand a response that goes beyond political slogans, mere rhetoric, and the constraints of traditional political allegiances.

Empathy in this context must be recognized as more than just a passive emotional response; it must be seen as an active force for change. It involves not only understanding the plight of others but also taking tangible steps to address injustices and inequalities. Empathy calls for a commitment to listen to diverse voices, to understand experiences different from our own, and to recognize the intrinsic value of every individual. This approach challenges us to look beyond our own perspectives and to see the world through the eyes of others.

Moreover, empathy must become a guiding principle in our public discourse and policy-making. It should inform how we address complex social issues, from poverty and inequality to racial and gender discrimination. By prioritising empathy, we can begin to dismantle the systemic barriers that perpetuate discrimination, fostering a more inclusive and equitable society.

To achieve this, a profound cultural shift is required. We must cultivate empathy in our education systems, encouraging young people to develop a deep understanding of and compassion for others. We must promote empathetic leadership, where decision-makers are guided by a genuine concern for the well-being of all members of society. In our everyday interactions, we must strive to practice empathy, making a conscious effort to understand and appreciate the experiences and perspectives of those around us.

The journey towards a more empathetic society is both challenging and essential. It requires us to move beyond the confines of traditional political discourse and to see the issues of social justice, equality, and human rights not as political tools but as fundamental human concerns. By placing empathy at the forefront of our collective efforts, we can begin to create a world where discrimination is confronted not with indifference or hostility, but with understanding, compassion, and a shared commitment to justice and equality.

Empathy is a win-win for all engaged. Everyone, at some point, faces challenges or hardships where they seek understanding and support. Empathy allows us to connect with others on a deeper level, fostering a society where people are more likely to help each other in times of need. Empathy opens the door to understanding diverse perspectives, which can lead to richer, more creative solutions in both personal and professional settings. A society that values different viewpoints is more innovative and adaptable. It enriches personal relationships, leading to stronger connections with friends, family, and colleagues. It allows individuals to develop deeper bonds based on mutual respect and understanding. Empathy contributes to emotional well-being, both for the giver and the receiver. Understanding and sharing the feelings of others can help reduce feelings of isolation and build a sense of community and belonging.

In many professional environments, empathy is increasingly recognized as a valuable skill. It can improve leadership abilities, enhance teamwork, and lead to better customer relations. Empathy plays a crucial role in resolving conflicts, both on a personal and societal level. By understanding the perspectives and feelings of others, it's easier to find common ground and work towards peaceful solutions. Societies that prioritize empathy often have stronger social support systems, leading to more stability and less social unrest. This stability can translate into economic benefits, such as higher productivity and more cooperative work environments. Being empathetic doesn't mean sacrificing one's own needs or values; it's about understanding and respecting the feelings of others. Empathy enriches one's life experience rather than diminishing it.

In the tapestry of contemporary society, the digital revolution has woven a complex and often troubling picture, particularly regarding the dissemination of information. This new landscape is marked by an intricate battle between truth and lies, a struggle profoundly intensified in the digital age. As we delve deeper into the subsequent chapters, it becomes evident that the rise of digital media, while bringing unprecedented access to information, has simultaneously unleashed a torrent of misinformation. This duality presents a significant challenge to the very fabric of our society and the integrity of our collective knowledge.

The proliferation of digital platforms has democratized information dissemination, allowing voices from all corners of the globe to be heard. However, this democratization has a darker side. It has also provided fertile ground for the spread of fake news, deepfakes, and 'alternative facts.' These tools of deception are not just mere inconveniences or harmless falsehoods. They are potent weapons in the hands of those with nefarious intentions, often wielded to manipulate public opinion, sow division, and undermine trust in facts and institutions.

This era of widespread deception is further exacerbated by the actions of certain elite groups and individuals who exploit social media networks for their own gain. By leveraging their resources and influence, these actors amplify the spread of misinformation, manipulating narratives to serve their interests. They exploit the algorithms and echo chambers inherent in social media platforms to create a distorted reality, where lies are perpetuated and truth becomes obscured.

The impact of this manipulation is far-reaching and deeply concerning. It erodes the foundation of informed decision-making in a democratic society, where citizens rely on accurate information to make choices about their leaders, policies, and the direction of their nation. The spread of misinformation breeds confusion and mistrust, weakening the very pillars of democracy.

Moreover, the misuse of social media by the elite raises profound ethical questions about the responsibility of technology companies and the need for regulation. These platforms once heralded as tools for freedom of expression and democratic engagement, are now seen as double-edged swords, capable of both enlightening and deceiving the public. The challenge lies in balancing the freedom of speech with the need to protect society from the deliberate spread of falsehoods.

As we explore this topic further in the following chapters, we will examine the various facets of this issue: the psychological and societal impacts of misinformation, the role of technology companies in curbing its spread, and the measures that can be taken to foster a more informed and discerning public. We will delve into the strategies employed by those in power to manipulate digital media and how society can resist and counteract these tactics.

The need for media literacy has never been more critical. In a world where the line between truth and falsehood is increasingly blurred, the ability to critically evaluate information sources, understand the motives behind certain messages and discern fact from fiction is paramount. This literacy is not just an individual responsibility but a collective one, requiring concerted efforts from educators, policymakers, media professionals, and the public at large.

The debate within the modern sociopolitical landscape is further complicated by a profound conflict that stretches beyond mere political ideology – it is the clash between the rigour of scientific inquiry and the murky realm of conspiracy theories. This conflict, as we will explore in depth in later chapters of this book, manifests itself in various critical global issues, revealing the stark contrast between evidence-based reasoning and the allure of unfounded speculation.

Science, anchored in evidence-based research and rigorous experimentation, is a beacon of truth and progress in a world filled with uncertainties. This disciplined pursuit of verifiable facts has been fundamental in advancing medicine, technology, and our comprehension of the natural world, taking humanity to new frontiers like space exploration and unravelling complex diseases.

In stark contrast stand conspiracy theories, often characterized by their reliance on unfounded suspicions and a blatant rejection of established knowledge. These theories thrive on the human tendency towards pattern recognition and storytelling, providing seemingly simple explanations for complex phenomena. However, such explanations frequently lack empirical evidence and logical coherence, instead relying on conjecture, hearsay, and often, the deliberate distortion of facts.

This dichotomy becomes particularly evident when examining contentious current issues like globalization, the dynamics of Brexit, the rise of authoritarianism in the US and globally, climate change, vaccinations, and the COVID-19 pandemic. Each of these topics represents an arena where the struggle between scientific understanding and conspiratorial thinking plays out with significant consequences.

For instance, in the context of globalization, conspiracy theories often misconstrue economic and cultural dynamics, promoting protectionist and isolationist sentiments. Similarly, the discourse surrounding Brexit was rife with misinformation and exaggerated claims, clouding the public's understanding of the European Union and the implications of leaving it.

The rise of authoritarianism, both in the United States and globally, has been fuelled in part by conspiracy theories that undermine trust in democratic institutions and processes. These theories are used as tools to manipulate public opinion, justify autocratic policies, and entrench power.

In the realm of environmental science, climate change stands as a critical issue where the denial of scientific consensus has significant global implications. Despite overwhelming evidence (by scientists from both sides of the vested interest spectrum) supporting human-driven climate change, conspiracy theories continue to sow doubt, hindering effective policy responses.

The fields of public health and medicine have not been immune to this conflict either. The anti-vaccination movement, bolstered by conspiracy theories, poses a direct challenge to public health initiatives, as seen in the response to the COVID-19 pandemic. Misinformation regarding the virus's origins, nature, and vaccines has led to public confusion, vaccine hesitancy, and resistance to health measures, exacerbating the crisis.

This conflict between science and conspiracy theories transcends mere political differences, revealing a deep divide in how people engage with evidence, expertise, and scientific understanding. It highlights a broader societal challenge: the need for critical thinking and media literacy in a world inundated with information of varying reliability.

As we proceed in this book, we will delve deeper into these issues, examining the roots of this divide and exploring ways to bridge the gap. We will look at how education, public outreach, and policy can be leveraged to promote a greater understanding of scientific principles and methods. Ultimately, our goal is to illuminate the path towards a society where decisions and beliefs are informed by evidence and reason, rather than fear and misinformation. This journey is crucial not only for addressing the immediate challenges posed by these issues but for the long-term health and well-being of our global community.

The Manipulation of Public Sentiment

Source: www.speedbump.com

The concentration of wealth within the top 1% has raised concerns about economic disparity and the erosion of the middle class. This phenomenon is not a mere accident but rather the result of deliberate manipulation, convincing a significant portion of the population to vote against their own economic interests. The elite 1% employs strategic communication and rhetorical tactics to sway public opinion, ensuring the preservation of their advantageous position.

Propaganda, as a formidable instrument, serves the 1% in spreading ideas and influencing public opinion. It enables them to craft narratives tailored to their interests, manipulating information to appeal to emotions and prejudices, making it challenging for ordinary citizens to make informed decisions.

Inflammatory rhetoric plays a critical role in sowing discord and resentment among the population. Through clever language use, the elite frames their policies as beneficial to all, while portraying policies supporting the majority as dangerous or unpatriotic. This divisive language effectively turns the electorate against policies aimed at promoting wealth equality and safeguarding the middle class.

The continuous assault on the 99% through propaganda and inflammatory rhetoric results in diminished economic prospects and stability. With the wealthy elite controlling the narrative, policies that could provide relief and opportunity for the 99% are often undermined or misrepresented. This perpetuates a cycle of economic disadvantage and disempowerment.

We shall now delve into the elusive ways through which the 1% exerts influence over the 99%. These manipulations subtly shift perceptions and attitudes to safeguard the elite's interests. Through strategically crafted messages disseminated across various media platforms, the elite induces divisions within the 99%, fostering a climate of resentment and competition amongst subgroups. This subliminal push glorifies wealth and individualism, steering society towards valuing affluence as a moral virtue and viewing poverty as a personal failure. Awareness and critical examination of these influences are pivotal for reclaiming agency, fostering solidarity, and advocating for a more equitable societal structure.

A crucial aspect to address is the subtle, often unnoticed influence the elite exerts on society's perceptions, beliefs, and attitudes. Subliminal influence refers to the stealthy manipulation techniques employed to sway public opinion and behavior without their explicit awareness.

The 1% utilizes various mediums to disseminate narratives that serve their interests, capitalizing on advertising, media outlets, and digital platforms. These messages are meticulously crafted, subtly promoting values and perspectives that align with the interests of the elite. The constant exposure to these covert signals fosters a social environment where the priorities and viewpoints of the 1% become deeply ingrained in the collective psyche of society.

The portrayal of social welfare programs as burdensome or depicting the unemployed and under-employed as dependent or unmotivated are narrative threads subtly woven into public discourse. This divisive strategy pits different subgroups within the 99% against each other, diluting the potential power of their collective action and solidarity.

Society is inundated with narratives that glorify wealth accumulation, success, and individualism as paramount values, often at the expense of community, solidarity, and shared responsibility. This subliminal message coerces the 99% to internalise and aspire towards these values, unwittingly creating a social environment where wealth is admired as a moral virtue. At the same time, poverty is associated with personal failure, deepening societal divisions.

A persistent narrative against labour unions is embedded within various communication channels. Unions, that advocate for workers' rights and equitable employment conditions, are often depicted as troublesome or corrupt. These viewpoints undermine these organizations' credibility, discouraging workers from unionizing or fighting collectively for their rights, indirectly preserving the 1%'s interests.

The subliminal messages and covert manipulation tactics deployed by the 1% have a profound impact on the 99%, shaping their perceptions, values, and actions in ways that exacerbate divisions and inequality within society. These influences subtly steer the majority away from recognizing their shared interests and collective power, eroding solidarity, fostering unrealistic expectations, and hindering the development of a fair societal structure. Recognizing and critically engaging with these covert messages is pivotal for the 99% to reclaim narrative control, challenge subtly imposed values, and foster a society based on fairness, empathy, and shared responsibility. Each example underscores the importance of vigilance and critical thinking in navigating a world steeped in subtle influences designed to uphold the status and power of the elite 1%.

The advent of digital technology and social media, primarily driven by middle-class innovators, has yielded a paradoxical outcome. These platforms, initially heralded for their potential to democratize information, have been harnessed with remarkable proficiency by the economic elite for propagating their narratives. While the 1% swiftly recognized the strategic value of digital tools and invested heavily in them, leveraging skilled professionals for marketing and psychological manipulation, the creators themselves often find their economic dependence on affluent entities inadvertently serving the interests of the elite. The lack of coordinated strategies and collective will among the middle class exacerbates this predicament.

Financial incentives and ethical desensitization further compound the issue, as lucrative opportunities from wealthy individuals or corporations can overshadow ethical considerations and lead to a normalization of data manipulation and misinformation for profit. To address this challenge, it is imperative to foster ethical awareness among tech professionals and the wider public, promoting responsible digital tool use. Equipping the middle class with collective digital literacy and the ability to discern misinformation is essential, along with the development and implementation of organized and effective counter-narratives to reposition these digital tools as assets for the broader society. The paradox of middle-class innovators falling victim to the misuse of their own inventions requires a concerted effort to reclaim and utilize digital platforms for the promotion of truth and the common good.

AI technology marks a turning point in the wealthy elite's campaign of influencing public perception. Through AI's analytical and generative capabilities, the 1% can now execute more sophisticated and impactful propaganda strategies, further eroding the economic position and political power of the middle class.

Populism's ascent as a significant political force is indeed a phenomenon of our times, influenced greatly by the advent of sophisticated data analytics, epitomized by firms like Cambridge Analytica and Facebook. These entities have leveraged advanced data analysis and targeted communication strategies to pinpoint and mobilize specific voter groups, often capitalizing on their discontent with the prevailing political landscape.

These strategies have empowered populist movements to forge broad coalitions, uniting diverse groups under a common (if not false) banner of shared grievances and disillusionment. This has brought about a notable transformation in political discourse. Populist movements frequently employ simplistic yet emotionally charged rhetoric, tapping into the deep-seated frustrations of voters and positioning themselves as the panacea to societal woes.

While effective in garnering support, this tactic has precipitated a rise in divisive and polarizing language, exacerbating societal divisions. The consequences of this shift are profound and far-reaching, posing risks to the fabric of democracy and societal stability.

To enhance this analysis, it's important to recognize the role of social media and digital platforms in amplifying populist messages, which we shall detail in the following pages. The digital age has provided an unprecedented arena for populist narratives to spread rapidly, often unfiltered and unchecked. This has facilitated a faster and more potent dissemination of populist ideas, contributing to the rapid growth and influence of these movements.

Furthermore, the impact on democratic institutions cannot be understated. The rise of populism, fueled by data-driven strategies and emotional appeals, has challenged the traditional mechanisms of political engagement and decision-making. It has often led to the oversimplification of complex policy issues and undermined the process of reasoned, evidence-based debate that is fundamental to democratic governance.

While the rise of populism and its data-driven strategies have reshaped the political landscape, they also underscore the need for robust democratic safeguards, informed citizen engagement, and responsible use of technology in the political arena.

AI algorithms meticulously analyze public opinion and societal trends, allowing the 1% to craft highly targeted and persuasive messages. These technologies can identify demographic groups susceptible to specific narratives, enabling the elite to:

Segment and Target

This involves micro-targeting specific groups with content meticulously crafted to resonate with their particular fears, hopes, and grievances. This strategy is finely tuned to exploit the unique vulnerabilities and aspirations of different segments of society, thereby maximizing its persuasive power. By feeding into the existing anxieties and dreams of these groups, this approach not only reinforces their current beliefs but subtly nudges them toward adopting viewpoints and making decisions that might not inherently align with their genuine interests or welfare. The precise nature of this tailored content makes it exceptionally potent, as it speaks directly to the individual concerns and desires of each targeted group, enhancing the likelihood of these messages being accepted and acted upon without critical scrutiny.

Optimize Messaging

This entails the continuous refinement and adaptation of propaganda to enhance its impact and persuasiveness, making it a fluid and dynamic tool for influencing public perception and behaviour. Through constant adjustments in response to shifting societal trends, public opinions, and emerging events, this approach ensures that the disseminated messages remain relevant, engaging, and convincing to the intended audiences. By analyzing the reception and effectiveness of each propaganda piece, proponents of this strategy can fine-tune their narratives, emphasizing elements that resonate strongly while minimizing or altering aspects that may hinder the propaganda's efficacy. This process of ongoing optimization creates a cycle of ever-improving, highly potent propaganda that effectively sways public opinion in the desired direction, often without the audience being consciously aware of the manipulation taking place.

Monitor Effectiveness

The immediate assessment of public responses to propaganda allows for prompt adjustments to strategies based on the feedback received. This approach is crucial for maintaining the efficacy and relevance of propaganda efforts. Real-time monitoring tools and analytics are deployed to observe how messages are being received and interpreted by the public, tracking metrics like engagement, sentiment, and spread. This instantaneous feedback allows propagandists to understand the impact of their narratives, identifying what works and what doesn't in engaging and persuading different audience segments. With this valuable insight, strategies can be recalibrated on the fly, ensuring that messages are continuously optimized to exert the most significant influence over public opinion and behaviour. Through this cycle of monitoring and adjustment, propagandists can craft more compelling and persuasive narratives that subtly guide audiences to adopt specific viewpoints and take desired actions.

AI for Disseminating Fake News and Conspiracy Theories

AI and advanced algorithms play a pivotal role in disseminating fake news and conspiracy theories, acting as powerful amplifiers for misinformation. These technologies are adept at identifying and targeting individuals and groups susceptible to specific types of false narratives, serving them content that aligns with their pre-existing beliefs and biases. By analyzing users' online behaviour, social connections, and content preferences, AI can craft and propagate messages that are highly likely to be accepted and shared by recipients, further entrenching their misconceptions and misguided views. Furthermore, AI-driven bots and automated accounts can artificially boost the prominence and perceived credibility of fake news and conspiracy theories, manipulating online discourse and swaying public opinion at scale. This high-tech approach to misinformation distribution enables precision and efficiency that is unparalleled, making AI a formidable tool in the arsenal of those looking to spread falsehoods and shape reality according to their agenda.

Content Generation

AI's capabilities in Content Generation are significantly sophisticated, allowing for the autonomous creation of compelling and often indistinguishable fake news articles, social media posts, and deepfake videos. By utilizing advanced algorithms and machine learning, AI can craft narratives that closely mimic the writing styles and tones found in legitimate news sources, creating misinformation that is not easily debunked or distinguished from the truth by unsuspecting readers. Similarly, deepfake technology enables the creation of highly convincing video content, wherein individuals appear to say or do things they never actually did, further blurring the lines between reality and fabrication. These AI-generated pieces of content can be tailored to appeal to specific audiences, reinforcing existing biases, sowing discord, and promoting agendas that may be harmful or misleading, all while operating at a scale and speed unattainable by human actors alone.

Automated Distribution

The age of Automated Distribution has given rise to bots and algorithms, potent tools that disseminate misinformation swiftly and on an unprecedented scale. These automated mechanisms operate efficiently, spreading fabricated narratives far and wide before traditional fact-checking and counter-narrative efforts can even begin to address the falsehoods. Bots tirelessly flood social media platforms and online forums with misleading information, while sophisticated algorithms ensure that this content reaches audiences most likely to be influenced. Together, they create a daunting environment where misinformation circulates uncontested, hindering the public's ability to discern truth from fabrication and undermining informed discourse and decision-making in the process.

Social Media Manipulation

Social Media Manipulation through AI serves as a powerful engine for artificially amplifying specific narratives, dramatically tilting the scales of public discourse and perception. Through sophisticated algorithms, AI can boost the visibility and apparent popularity of chosen messages, making them seem more widely accepted or debated than they truly are. This form of manipulation plays a crucial role in shaping online dialogues, as it creates a false consensus or a sense of urgency around particular topics or viewpoints. Consequently, individuals encountering these amplified messages are more likely to be influenced, believing they represent the prevailing opinion or a significant trend, which can distort collective understanding and decision-making in society. The artificial inflation of certain narratives, therefore, not only misrepresents the informational landscape but also plays a decisive role in steering public conversations and sentiments in specific, often misleading, directions.

By dividing and Conquering the Middle Class by exploiting AI's capabilities, the 1% can:

Intensify Divisions

AI-driven tools are adeptly employed to intensify societal divisions, effectively driving wedges into the existing cracks of social cohesion. By artificially inflaming societal animosities and divisions, attention is strategically diverted away from pressing issues like wealth inequality and corporate wrongdoing. Techniques include the amplification of extremist views, polarization of opinions, and exacerbation of identity-based conflicts, all conducted with the precise aim of fostering an environment of discord and distraction. In this turbulent atmosphere, public focus is shifted, and crucial conversations regarding the wealth gap and corporate accountability are overshadowed by rising tides of internal conflict and animosity among divergent social groups, allowing the elite to further consolidate wealth and power unscrutinized and unopposed.

Undermine Trust
AI can be employed as a powerful tool to systematically undermine public trust in institutions and information sources that pose a threat to the narratives carefully crafted by the elite. Through the calculated distribution of misinformation and propaganda, these technological tools sow seeds of confusion and scepticism among the populace. This destabilizes the credibility of organizations and media outlets traditionally seen as reliable, causing individuals to question the legitimacy of the information they present. As trust erodes, society becomes fragmented and more susceptible to accepting alternative narratives that align with the interests of the elite. This atmosphere of distrust and uncertainty not only facilitates the manipulation of public opinion but also incapacitates the ability of society to collectively challenge or counteract the deceptive narratives propagated by those in power.

Manipulate Behavior

Sophisticated AI technologies have been weaponized to stealthily manipulate public behaviour, swaying opinions and voting patterns in ways that subtly favour policies and candidates meticulously aligned with the interests of the 1%. This covert influence operates beneath the radar, deploying an array of advanced algorithms and data analytics tools to craft messages that resonate deeply with targeted segments of the populace. These messages, often hyper-personalized, are strategically designed to evoke emotional responses, steering individuals towards adopting viewpoints and making electoral choices that they believe are independently reasoned, but are in fact, outcomes orchestrated by the invisible hand of elite influence. The endgame of these manipulative practices is the creation of a political landscape where elected officials and policies systematically tilt towards safeguarding and promoting the wealth and power of the elite minority, often at the expense of the broader 99%.

The insidious nature of AI, big data, and social media targeting in modern political campaigns presents a significant and stealthy challenge to democracy and informed public discourse. These technologies, while innovative, have been weaponised to manipulate public opinion through highly personalized and targeted strategies. The narrow focus of this targeting means that most people remain unaware of the specific tactics, advertisements, and manipulative techniques being used, as these are often tailored to individual profiles and therefore not visible to the broader public.

This lack of visibility and awareness creates an environment where counter-campaigns struggle to effectively address or debunk the misinformation being spread. The personalized nature of the content makes it difficult to monitor and counteract, as each individual receives a unique set of messages based on their online behaviour, preferences, and demographic data. This can lead to a fragmented understanding of political issues among the populace, as different groups or individuals are exposed to vastly different narratives.

Policymakers and technology companies must collaborate to establish ethical guidelines and regulatory frameworks for the use of personal data in political campaigns. This includes ensuring user consent for data collection, limiting the types of data that can be used for political targeting, and creating mechanisms for accountability and oversight.

In summary, the sophisticated use of AI, big data, and social media in political targeting poses a significant threat to the integrity of democratic processes. Combating this threat requires a multi-faceted approach, involving increased public awareness, regulatory oversight, and a commitment to ethical standards in the use of technology in politics. Only through these measures can we safeguard democratic discourse and ensure that technology serves to enhance, rather than undermine, the foundations of our democratic societies.

For a better understanding of the utilisation of these tools by the 1%, read the chapter on BREXIT.

The Capitalism Conundrum

Over the past half-century, the top 1% have played a significant role in shaping economic policy, fostering wealth inequality, and eroding the middle class. Concurrently, they've shifted the blame for economic woes onto socialist ideologies, effectively manipulating the public to vote against their interests. This chapter examines these manipulative strategies and their impacts.

The elite 1% have subtly engineered an economic landscape where wealth accumulates at the top, primarily through suppressing wages and advocating for policies that favour their accumulation of wealth. This strategic economic manipulation has not only widened the wealth gap but has also methodically disempowered and shrunk the middle class.

While engaging in practices that exacerbate wealth inequality, the 1% have simultaneously waged a propaganda war against socialism. Through meticulously crafted narratives, they've positioned socialism as the enemy of prosperity, effectively diverting attention from the capitalist practices that they have wielded to consolidate wealth and power.

By controlling the economic narrative, the 1% have managed to sway public opinion against socialism and other wealth-redistributive policies. Their carefully executed campaigns play on fears and misconceptions, painting socialism as a threat to individual freedoms and capitalist success, even as the middle class continues to suffer under the weight of these capitalist practices.

While this chapter delves into politics to illuminate how the 1% utilize lobbyists to sidetrack beneficial government policies, it is not intended to endorse either political side. Instead, it illustrates how subtle messaging and media manipulation can lead the 99% to unknowingly champion and vote for agendas contrary to their own interests.

The 1% often uses specific terms, phrases, and "bogeymen" as tools to shift blame and deflect attention away from the economic inequality they perpetuate. Some of these are outlined below:

Socialism

The term is frequently used pejoratively to instil fear of wealth redistribution and government overreach, often misrepresented as a system that stifles innovation, entrepreneurship, and economic growth; even as corporations turn to governments and tax dollars for bailouts due to their bad management decisions!

Socialism refers to an economic and political system where the means of production, distribution, and exchange are owned or regulated by the community. While there are various forms of socialism, the Nordic model offers valuable insights. Nordic countries like Sweden, Norway, and Denmark invest in robust social safety nets, providing universal healthcare, free education, and unemployment benefits.

These nations implement progressive tax policies, ensuring that the wealthy contribute a fair share, facilitating wealth redistribution and funding for public services. Key sectors, such as healthcare and utilities, are often publicly owned or regulated, ensuring accessibility and affordability for all citizens.

While the U.S. operates under a capitalist system, incorporating socialist principles (while remaining a fully functioning if not equitable democracy), could address several societal challenges. A universal healthcare system would guarantee access to medical services for all Americans, regardless of their economic status. Investing in free or subsidized higher education would empower more individuals to pursue advanced degrees without incurring crippling debt. Progressive taxation and robust social safety nets would mitigate income inequality and provide a security blanket for unemployed and underemployed citizens.

The 1% has engaged in a systematic campaign to distort the understanding of socialism. The elite often equate socialism with authoritarian regimes, intentionally ignoring the successes of democratic socialist countries. By framing socialism as antithetical to freedom and prosperity, the 1% stoke unfounded fears of government overreach and economic decline. The affluent selectively highlight failed socialist states while ignoring the achievements of successful socialist nations to create a skewed perception of socialism's viability and benefits.

Nordic countries are smaller than the U.S., but this doesn't inherently mean their systems are unscalable. Large populations can benefit from economies of scale in public services. The real challenge is in the effective implementation and adaptation of these systems to other contexts, not in the size of the population itself. This diversity is often cited as a reason why certain policies may not be as effective. However, this diversity also brings a wide range of ideas and innovations that can be harnessed to make adapted systems work effectively.

There's a need to clarify misconceptions about Nordic socialism. Nordic countries practice a form of social democracy, which combines free market capitalism with a strong welfare state. This is different from socialism as traditionally defined. Other countries can explore a similar blend of capitalism with enhanced social welfare policies. There are examples of larger nations successfully implementing policies often associated with Nordic models, such as universal healthcare or subsidized education. These examples demonstrate that size is not an insurmountable obstacle.

Concerns about the fiscal feasibility of such systems in a larger country like the U.S. need to be addressed. This involves discussing potential funding sources, such as tax reforms, and the long-term economic benefits of a healthier, more educated population. An incremental approach to implementing Nordic-style policies can be a practical response, gradually introducing and testing policies at state or local levels can provide insights and data to guide a larger-scale implementation.

The growing economic inequality in certain democracies and the potential of Nordic-style policies to mitigate these issues are compelling. These policies aim to provide a more level playing field, which is a concern that resonates with many in countries like America.

Welfare State

It's used to conjure images of a government that excessively coddles its citizens, fostering dependency and laziness while draining public funds.

The term "welfare state" refers to a governmental system where the state plays a key role in protecting and promoting the social and economic well-being of its citizens, primarily through social security, unemployment insurance, and public services. Countries with robust welfare states invest heavily in their citizens, offering support like universal healthcare, education, housing assistance, and unemployment benefits. The welfare state aims to mitigate income inequality and provide a baseline standard of living, promoting a more equitable society.

Countries with strong welfare provisions, such as those in Scandinavia and Western Europe, demonstrate the viability and benefits of this system. With access to free or affordable education and healthcare, citizens have greater opportunities to improve their socio-economic status. Welfare systems act as economic stabilizers during downturns, providing support to individuals and families and maintaining consumer spending.

The welfare state is often misrepresented by wealthy elites. The 1% perpetuates the myth that welfare fosters dependency and laziness among recipients, discouraging work and personal responsibility. They also argue that welfare programs are financially unsustainable, draining public resources and imposing burdens on taxpayers and businesses.

Empirical evidence from successful welfare states demonstrates that these systems can encourage work, education, and social participation while offering necessary support. A healthy, educated, and secure populace contributes positively to the economy, fostering a more productive and stable society. Publicizing the achievements and benefits of welfare states can counter negative stereotypes and provide a more balanced view of their potential.

The welfare state, despite being portrayed as a system that fosters dependency and economic strain, is a proven model that offers myriad social and economic benefits.

Tax and Spend Progressives
This phrase aims to paint progressive politicians and their policies as financially irresponsible, implying they recklessly impose high taxes and waste money on impractical social programs.

The phrase "tax and spend" progressives are commonly used to stereotype left-leaning politicians who advocate for higher taxes on the wealthy and increased public spending on social services. Progressives often aim to direct taxes towards improving public services, infrastructure, education, and healthcare, which are crucial for societal welfare. They endorse a tax structure where the wealthy pay a fair share, supporting the economic system that allows their wealth accumulation. Countries employing progressive taxation and higher public spending often enjoy high living standards and social stability:

Again, Nordic countries, known for their higher and fair taxes, boast strong economies, low-income inequality, and high-quality public services. Progressive tax policies provide consistent revenue for essential services without compromising economic growth or stability.

The 1% paints liberals as reckless with public funds, accusing them of wasting taxpayer money without providing tangible benefits. They claim that progressive tax policies disincentivize investment and innovation, purportedly leading to economic decline.

However, under Bill Clinton's presidency (1993-2001), the United States witnessed substantial economic growth, decreased unemployment rates, and eventually achieved a budget surplus. Clinton's administration endorsed policies promoting investment and entrepreneurship, with a simultaneous focus on deficit reduction and the enhancement of social welfare programs. This approach mirrored the economic strategy observed in Nordic countries, where investment in social welfare not only supports citizens but also fosters a robust economy.

The Obama administration (2009-2017) navigated the challenge of the Great Recession with a series of fiscal stimulus packages and pivotal financial reforms. These efforts not only breathed life into a stagnating economy but also laid the groundwork for the Affordable Care Act (ACA). The ACA extended healthcare coverage to millions while controlling the growth of healthcare costs, reflecting the universal healthcare models successfully implemented in Nordic nations, which ensure that all citizens have access to quality healthcare without imposing financial hardship.

States governed by progressive leaders, such as California under Governors Jerry Brown and Gavin Newsom, have also exhibited fiscal responsibility while supporting social services, reminiscent of Nordic economic models that combine social welfare with fiscal prudence. These states have shown budget surpluses and significant investments in education, healthcare, and environmental initiatives. In evaluating fiscal responsibility, the context of inherited economic conditions must be considered. Progressive administrations often enter office during economic downturns, and while their policies might initially increase deficits, they lay the groundwork for long-term economic stability and growth, similar to the sustained economic success observed in Nordic countries.

President Biden's administration has seen a string of positive economic indicators, including cooling inflation, robust job growth, increased business investment, and an uptick in consumer and voter economic optimism, attributed in part to impactful legislation such as infrastructure, manufacturing, and climate bills. The economy experienced a 2.4 percent growth rate in the second quarter, outperforming expectations, while inflation slowed, and consumer spending increased. Notably, manufacturing has witnessed a considerable boost, with data showing a nearly 80 per cent increase in spending on manufacturing facilities compared to the previous year, resulting in the addition of approximately 800,000 jobs in the sector.

There are tangible economic improvements, such as the combination of subdued inflation, low unemployment rates, and wage growth, collectively enhancing the living standards of American workers. The American Rescue Plan, a $1.9 trillion stimulus package enacted by Biden, is acknowledged for sustaining consumer spending and business operations, thereby facilitating a rapid economic recovery characterized by low unemployment rates. While challenges and risks remain, the current economic landscape, marked by steady growth, low unemployment, and easing inflation, paints an optimistic picture, with forecasters increasingly hopeful about the U.S. averting a recession.

It's crucial to acknowledge that progressive governments, while not flawless, have had their fair share of achievements, and conservative administrations have also seen success. The label of "tax and spend" often attributed to liberals inaccurately depicts them as fiscally irresponsible—a narrative often advanced by wealthy interest groups aiming to undermine progressive economic agendas. By critically examining and debunking this narrative, and highlighting the triumphs of nations that have embraced progressive fiscal policies, we can shift the conversation towards advocating for economic approaches that prioritize the well-being of all citizens, rather than exclusively benefiting the elite.

Big Government

The term "Big Government" is often deployed to perpetuate the notion that extensive government involvement in the economy and the lives of individuals is inherently detrimental, stifling, and inefficient. This phrase is typically used to foster a negative view of policies and initiatives aimed at social welfare, environmental protection, and economic regulation, suggesting that such governmental oversight limits personal freedoms and hampers market efficiency. Advocates of smaller governments capitalize on this term to promote a vision of governance that minimizes regulation and intervention, often at the expense of social safety nets and public goods, underscoring a philosophical divide on the role of government in society.

Death Tax

The term "Death Tax" is a sensationalized label for the estate tax, ingeniously crafted to incite opposition to taxes levied on substantial inheritances passed down through generations. By evoking the notion of undue taxation during a time of familial grief and loss, this term manipulates public sentiment, framing the tax as an unfair burden on bereaved families. In reality, the estate tax affects a minute fraction of the population—specifically, those inheriting considerable wealth. Consequently, the narrative surrounding the so-called "Death Tax" often obscures its impact, which predominantly falls on the most affluent segments of society, while it serves as a crucial revenue source that can fund essential public services and contribute to mitigating wealth inequality.

Job Killers

The phrase "Job Killers" is frequently deployed as a rhetorical weapon against regulations, labour laws, or progressive policies that are designed to protect workers, consumers, and the environment. This term implies that such measures inadvertently stifle business growth and employment opportunities. However, a closer examination reveals that this characterization is often misleading or oversimplified. Many policies labelled as "Job Killers" actually contribute to creating more sustainable, equitable, and stable economic conditions in the long run. For instance, while certain regulations might necessitate adjustments or incur costs for businesses, they often lead to the emergence of new industries and jobs, promote fair working conditions, and foster a healthier, more productive workforce. It's imperative to scrutinize the "Job Killers" narrative critically, considering the broader and more nuanced socio-economic impacts of the policies in question.

Radical Left or Extreme Left

The terms "Radical Left" or "Extreme Left" are often used pejoratively to portray left-leaning individuals or groups as dangerous, un-democratic, or out of touch with so-called "mainstream" values. These labels tend to oversimplify and marginalize nuanced policy positions, casting any progressive or liberal idea as inherently threatening or irrational. They are commonly deployed to stigmatize proposals aimed at addressing income inequality, promoting social justice, or safeguarding civil rights, framing these initiatives as drastic or destabilizing. In reality, many proposals attributed to the "Radical" or "Extreme" Left often enjoy broad public support and aim to redress systemic issues that impact a significant portion of the population. It's crucial to approach these terms with a critical mindset, acknowledging their use as rhetorical devices meant to polarize, rather than illuminate, public discourse.

Class Warfare

The term "Class Warfare" is strategically employed to frame any attempts to address income inequality as divisive and malicious. This phrase suggests that initiatives aimed at wealth redistribution inherently pit different income groups against each other in a zero-sum conflict. For instance, when policies are proposed to adjust tax rates for higher income brackets or corporations to fund public services, critics may deploy the

"Class Warfare" narrative to imply that such measures are borne out of envy or animosity towards the wealthy. However, advocates of these policies often emphasize fairness, social cohesion, and economic justice rather than fostering division. They argue that adjusting tax structures can facilitate investment in essential public services and infrastructure that benefit society at large, contributing to a more equitable and stable social fabric where opportunity is accessible to all, regardless of their economic standing.

Entitlement Programs

The term "Entitlement Programs" is often used pejoratively to undermine the value of crucial social services that many societies provide, such as pension plans, healthcare provision, and income support for those in need. Critics who use this term imply that recipients of these benefits feel unduly "entitled" to these supports, painting a picture of ungrateful or lazy individuals exploiting the system at the expense of hardworking taxpayers. This narrative, however, overlooks the fundamental principle of social solidarity and collective responsibility that underpins these programs in many nations. The term also ignores the fact that these supports are not handouts but are often earned benefits that people have contributed to throughout their working lives, or they are safety nets designed to protect the most vulnerable in society from falling into abject poverty. Rather than fostering a sense of entitlement, these programs reflect a society's commitment to ensuring a dignified life for all citizens, recognizing that everyone can face periods of vulnerability or hardship at different points in their lives.

Unfunded Liabilities

"This is a term frequently deployed to describe social programs, casting them as financially unsustainable and burdensome for the economy. This framing serves to evoke alarm and concern among taxpayers, insinuating that these crucial initiatives are economically reckless and are precariously promised without adequate funding to back them. While it is indeed imperative to meticulously plan and secure financing for social programs, the term "unfunded liabilities" often unfairly disregards the long-term social and economic benefits these programs yield, including poverty alleviation, enhanced public health, and overall societal stability and well-being. The phrase also neglects the possibility of adjusting funding mechanisms and revenue streams, such as progressive taxation or closing tax loopholes, to sustainably finance these indispensable programs. Using "unfunded liabilities" as a blanket term oversimplifies the nuanced fiscal dynamics and planning involved in social programming, often with the aim of undermining support for these vital public services.

In this chapter, we have spotlighted specific terms that elites often employ subliminally to tarnish concepts inherently meant to benefit the vast majority of people, the 99%. If you notice yourself using these terms negatively, it's worth taking a moment to reflect. Consider: Where did these ideas originate? Are these beliefs truly yours, or might they have been subtly implanted by others? And if they were, who might have done so, and for what purpose? Upon reflection, you might discover that we can unwittingly become agents for those who aim to exploit us for their own gain and greed. These individuals or groups skillfully manipulate language and ideas, subtly influencing us to act in ways that ultimately serve their interests, not ours.

The Paradox of 'Citizens United' in American Democracy

Has democracy been mortally wounded by money in politics?

In the seemingly harmonious phrase "Citizens United," one might envision an idyllic portrait of national unity and solidarity. To the uninformed, it suggests an image of citizens collectively engaging in the democratic process, a representation of civic action and grassroots movements working towards societal change and progress. The phrase, on its surface, appears to embody the very essence of democratic empowerment and active participation, resonating with a spirit of communal strength and civic responsibility.

However, the stark reality unveiled by the 2010 Supreme Court ruling in Citizens United v. FEC presents a jarring contrast to this idealistic image. Far from promoting egalitarian unity, the decision paved the way for corporations and other entities to channel unlimited funds into political communications, dismantling previous restrictions. Ostensibly grounded in the First Amendment's principle of free speech, this ruling has sparked intense debate and polarized the American political landscape, criticized for disproportionately amplifying the influence of corporations and the wealthy elite in politics.

This contentious decision has profoundly impacted American politics, igniting debates over the role of money and the balance between free speech and campaign finance regulations. Critics of the ruling argue that it has opened floodgates for corruption, undermining the democratic process by allowing a surge of corporate funds to drown out individual voices. While the Supreme Court's decision was rooted in constitutional principles, it is argued that it failed to consider the potential for corruption and the erosion of democratic norms.

Attempts to mitigate the effects of Citizens United, such as the DISCLOSE Act, which calls for more transparency in political spending, have yet to succeed. The ruling remains a hotly debated topic, with arguments from both sides about the appropriate balance between free speech and fair campaign finance practices.

The Citizens United ruling has been a significant source of contention among legal scholars, political scientists, and activists. For many, the term "contentious" scarcely captures the depth and breadth of its implications on the political landscape. The ruling is often seen as a deviation from the principles of fairness and transparency that underpin the U.S. political system, with concerns that it skews the playing field in favour of wealthy interests, eroding public trust in politics.

Since the ruling, there has been a noticeable increase in political spending by corporations and wealthy individuals, leading to a widened gap between these entities and the average voter. The ruling serves as a sobering reminder of how law, with all its good intentions, can have unforeseen consequences that significantly shape the course of history.

In summary, the Citizens United ruling has contributed to a perception that the U.S. political system favours the wealthy and well-connected, challenging the foundational democratic promise of equal representation. It underscores a critical challenge faced by many democracies throughout history, requiring ongoing vigilance and engagement from citizens to ensure that their voices are heard and their interests represented. The chapter thus calls for a reevaluation of the role of money in politics and a reaffirmation of the democratic values of fairness and transparency.

In Switzerland, known for its direct democracy, there has been criticism for a lack of transparency in political financing. Unlike the U.S., Switzerland does not have clear rules on political campaign funding, leading to concerns about wealthy interests influencing political platforms. Recent legislative efforts aim to increase transparency, but progress has been slow, indicating a cautious approach towards regulating political financing.

However, The Swiss referenda system is a hallmark of direct democracy, providing a unique mechanism for citizens to have a direct impact on their country's laws and policies. This system is renowned for its emphasis on transparency and the empowerment of the people, ensuring that citizens play a central role in the decision-making process. This potentially offsets the lack of transparency in political private financing.

In the Nordic countries, political party finance is characterized by a heavy reliance on public subsidies and efforts towards transparency. For instance, Sweden's political parties derive a significant portion of their income from public funding, and recent legislative initiatives aim to make information regarding the funding of political parties more accessible. This model contrasts with the U.S. system by reducing the influence of private money and ensuring a level playing field.

Within the EU, member states have their own sets of rules and practices regarding campaign finance, generally aimed at promoting fair political competition and curbing the influence of money over politics. These regulations often include rules on contributions, expenditures, disclosure requirements, and sanctions, reflecting a commitment to balance and transparency in political financing.

The UK's approach to campaign finance, governed by the Political Parties, Elections, and Referendums Act 2000, sets clear rules on political donations and spending, with an emphasis on transparency and fairness. Unlike the U.S., the UK has strict limits on both donations and campaign spending, and corporations are subject to the same restrictions as individual donors. The Electoral Commission actively enforces these laws, ensuring compliance and addressing violations.

Determining which system works best to protect against the influence of money in politics depends on various factors, including the effectiveness of regulations, the level of transparency, and the overall political culture. While no system is perfect, the Nordic model and the UK's approach stand out for their combination of public funding, strict regulations, transparency, and active enforcement. These elements contribute to reducing the undue influence of private money in politics and maintaining a fair and democratic political process.

I hold a strong preference for the Swiss system of referenda, which is poised to grow even more robust as the country progresses towards enhanced transparency in political funding. A notable illustration of this system's effectiveness is seen in Zurich, Switzerland's largest canton, where a recent referendum had a resounding outcome. In this referendum, voters decisively approved a new measure aimed at fostering cleaner and more efficient resource utilization. An impressive 90% of Zurich's electorate, casting their votes, endorsed this proposal put forward by the cantonal government. Significantly, this initiative received unanimous support from all political parties.

This outcome is not just a reflection of the policy's merit but also a testament to the discernment and maturity of the Swiss citizenry. It demonstrates that the voters in Zurich are not easily influenced or misled by deceptive tactics or falsehoods propagated by groups with vested interests. Instead, they show a commendable ability to make informed decisions based on sound scientific principles and objectives. This inclination towards science-based decision-making underscores the strength and sophistication of Switzerland's democratic processes, particularly in the context of referenda.

The Zurich referendum's outcome highlights the efficacy of Switzerland's education system in cultivating an informed and discerning citizenry. Known for its high quality and comprehensive approach, Swiss education emphasizes not just academic learning but also critical thinking, civic education, and the development of well-rounded individuals. Students are encouraged to engage with a broad range of subjects, including sciences, humanities, and social sciences, fostering a balanced understanding of the world and promoting critical thinking skills. This educational approach results in a populace capable of informed decision-making and critical analysis.

Furthermore, Swiss education places a strong emphasis on civic education, teaching students extensively about democratic principles, active citizenship, and the significance of referenda in their political system. This early and continued focus on civic responsibility ensures that citizens are well-versed in their country's political processes and the importance of their participation. Additionally, the Swiss educational system's emphasis on vocational training and apprenticeships, alongside traditional academic pathways, ensures inclusivity and access to quality education for all citizens, contributing to a broadly informed electorate.

In contrast, the U.S. education system often centers more on standardized testing and academic performance in core subjects. While critical thinking is valued, the focus on standardized tests can sometimes limit the scope for developing these skills. The curriculum varies significantly across states and districts, leading to variability in educational quality and focus. Civic education is part of the curriculum but its depth and effectiveness vary. In some cases, the focus on civics is less comprehensive, which may result in lower awareness of the political system and citizen responsibilities. Additionally, while vocational education is available in the U.S., it is often perceived as an alternative to academic pathways, primarily for students not pursuing college education.

These differences in education systems contribute to how citizens in each country engage with their democracy. In Switzerland, the combination of comprehensive civic education and societal emphasis on communal responsibility leads to a well-informed citizenry actively participating in direct democracy. In contrast, in the U.S., variability in educational quality and civic education, combined with a more individualistic societal ethos, might contribute to less uniform political engagement and understanding among the populace.

The disparities in educational funding between Switzerland and the U.S. also play a significant role. Switzerland invests heavily in its education system with significant public funding, ensuring high-quality education and equal access. In contrast, in the U.S., the reliance on local property taxes for funding education leads to disparities in educational resources and contributes to unequal educational opportunities. These factors influence not just the quality of education but also how effectively these systems prepare citizens for active and informed participation in democratic processes.

The Distortion of Empathy

In recent years, empathy, one of the core facets of human compassion, has undergone a transformation. It has been weaponized, rebranded as 'wokeness,' and strategically deployed as a divisive tool. This chapter will explore the multifaceted aspects of 'wokeness,' how it is employed for political purposes, its far-reaching impacts, and the benefits it affords politicians and the 1% in their quest to divide and conquer.

'Wokeness,' originally born from a desire for social awareness, compassion, and justice, has evolved into a term fraught with controversy. Its initial noble goals included addressing systemic inequalities, discrimination, and social injustices. However, the term has been co-opted and weaponized for political ends.

'Wokeness' was initially a response to centuries of systemic oppression, discrimination, and injustice faced by marginalized communities. It sought to raise awareness about these issues, promote empathy, and foster positive change. However, over time, it has become a catch-all term used to criticize any form of social awareness or advocacy, often caricaturing it as excessive sensitivity or political correctness.

Politicians and interest groups have strategically exploited the concept of 'wokeness' to create divisions within society. By framing social awareness and empathy as excessive sensitivity or political correctness, they capitalize on the backlash against these ideals. This serves their interests by diverting attention from pressing economic issues and consolidating their power.

The political exploitation of 'wokeness' is a deliberate strategy to polarize society. It allows politicians to rally their base by framing empathy and social justice as divisive forces threatening traditional values. By casting themselves as defenders of these values, they can distract from important economic debates and maintain their grip on power.

The term "wokeness" has undergone significant evolution in its meaning and usage over the years. Originally, "woke" emerged within African American Vernacular English (AAVE) and was associated with social and political awareness, particularly regarding issues of racial justice. Its roots can be traced back to the early 20th century, but it gained more prominent usage in the 1960s and 1970s, particularly in the context of the Civil Rights Movement.

The modern usage of "woke" as a broader term encompassing awareness of social and political injustices beyond just racial issues gained momentum in the 2010s. This shift was partly propelled by the Black Lives Matter movement, which emerged in 2013 after the acquittal of George Zimmerman in the shooting death of African-American teen Trayvon Martin. The hashtag #StayWoke became a rallying cry to remain vigilant against racial injustices.

The co-opting of "wokeness" into a term used pejoratively to describe a perceived overemphasis on political correctness or social justice issues, however, is a more recent phenomenon. It gained traction particularly among conservative commentators and political figures. This shift in meaning seems to have accelerated around the mid-2010s, becoming more pronounced towards the end of the decade.

Prominent figures in media and politics have played a role in this co-optation. They have used "woke" and "wokeness" to critique what they perceive as excessive sensitivity, overreach in social activism, or the policing of language and behavior in the name of social justice. This pejorative use of "wokeness" has become a common feature in political and cultural debates, often employed to dismiss or ridicule progressive stances on various social issues.

In summary, "wokeness" was co-opted from a term of awareness and vigilance against injustice, particularly in the African American community, to a term used to criticize certain aspects of progressive activism. This shift was not the result of a single individual's efforts but rather a broader cultural and political development, especially prominent among conservative commentators in the mid to late 2010s.

The exploitation of 'wokeness' has eroded solidarity within the middle class, a demographic crucial for social and political change. Internal divisions weaken collective action and make it easier for the economic elite to implement policies that disproportionately favour them. These policies include tax breaks for the wealthy, deregulation, and the undermining of workers' rights.

Middle-class divisions also hinder the development of a cohesive political agenda that addresses the economic challenges faced by the majority. Instead, energy is expended on debating cultural and social issues, which may be important but are often used as distractions from pressing economic concerns.

For politicians, the 'wokeness' critique offers a convenient distraction from addressing economic inequality. It allows them to rally their base by framing empathy and social justice as divisive forces threatening traditional values. In doing so, they secure their voter base and maintain their grip on political power.

The 1% benefits from these divisions as well. A fragmented middle class is less likely to unite in advocating for policies that challenge the status quo, such as progressive taxation or increased workers' rights. This maintains the concentration of wealth and power in the hands of the elite, perpetuating economic inequality.

The manipulation of empathy, framed as 'wokeness,' represents a complex and divisive phenomenon with far-reaching implications. Its emergence as a political tool has significant consequences for middle-class solidarity and the power dynamics within society. By understanding the motivations behind this manipulation and actively working to reframe empathy in a positive light, we can strive for a more united and equitable society that prioritizes compassion, justice, and cooperation over division and discord. The journey toward reclaiming empathy and its rightful place in our society is ongoing, but it is a path worth pursuing for the betterment of all.

Decoding Populism. A Case Study

In this Chapter, we invite you to engage deeply with the dissection and analysis of populism, understanding its real-world manifestations and impacts through case studies that spotlight climate change denial, misinformation during the COVID-19 pandemic, and ethical concerns related to AI development.

Populist leaders often propagate conspiracy theories as tools of persuasion, cultivating doubt and mistrust amongst the populace while simultaneously justifying policies that may not serve public interests. For example, in the context of the global health crisis, populist governance in some countries resulted in the dismissal of scientific expertise and promotion of unfounded theories, leading to some of the world's highest death rates due to the virus. In contrast, nations adhering to scientific guidelines, effectively manage and safeguard their citizens' health and well-being.

Further, as AI emerges as a potent force in modern society, populist regimes often adopt nationalistic approaches to this technology, raising serious ethical and human rights concerns as AI is potentially exploited for election manipulation, surveillance and control. These conspiracy-laden narratives about national security and technological sovereignty hinder collaborative efforts to establish global ethical standards and governance structures for AI.

These case studies, offer a nuanced understanding of how populism operates in practice, helping you decipher the subtle, and often detrimental, ways in which it shapes responses to global challenges, influences public opinion, and affects policy-making. With this foundation, you will be better equipped to critically assess populist narratives and advocate for leadership and policies that genuinely support the global community's collective well-being and future.

The global emergence of populist narratives is viewed with a discerning eye, as there's speculation regarding its origination and initial funding, with some suspicions pointing towards Russian financial backing. The populist narrative, as observed in various global contexts, taps into the deep-seated frustrations and anxieties of the masses. It constructs a seemingly anti-elite discourse that, in reality, serves as a smokescreen for the activities of the true elites, who discreetly orchestrate and benefit from the populist surge. In cases observed, these elites "select" and financially back charismatic populist figures who vocally oppose 'corrupt' establishments while subtly serving the interests of their hidden benefactors.

Under this alleged model, similar to the dynamic observed with Russian oligarchs and their relationship with political power, the financial elites meticulously support populist leaders promising to dismantle 'corrupt' systems. These figures, often with magnetic if not divisive personalities, offer deceptively simple solutions to complex societal issues. They serve as effective vehicles for the implementation of policies that favour the wealthy, pushing for tax reductions for the affluent, corporate deregulation, and the weakening of essential social safety nets.

This meticulously crafted populist narrative is a double-edged sword. On one side, it appears to advocate for the disenfranchised; on the other, it subtly advances an agenda that exacerbates wealth and power disparities. By manipulating the fears and grievances of the 99%, it diverts their discontent away from systemic issues, channelling it towards divisive, often xenophobic, ends.

Here, we delve into the rationality and subsequent impacts of populism, illustrating a complex phenomenon where the emotionally charged appeal often overshadows a careful and reasoned assessment of the consequences it yields. Populism, in its essence, is a reaction to genuine discontent within society; a voice to the frustrations, fears, and grievances of the 99%. However, as dissected in the previous discussions, it's crucial to understand that its expression and utilization often serve the hidden interests of the elite 1%.

The rationality behind populism lies in its ability to resonate with the masses by simplifying complex issues into digestible, albeit reductionist, messages. It often presents a binary worldview: 'the people' versus 'the elite', 'us' against 'them'. While this narrative strikes a chord with individuals who feel left behind or unheard, it is often manipulated by the true elites to consolidate power, as we explored in the suspected backing and crafting of populist narratives worldwide.

Populism impacts societies profoundly, creating waves of polarization and division. Its simplistic narratives can undermine democratic institutions, erode civil discourse, and perpetuate a culture of resentment and scapegoating. While promising empowerment, it often leads to the concentration of power in the hands of a few, paradoxically disempowering the very people it claims to represent. It tends to favour policies that, while popular, are short-sighted and ultimately detrimental to the socio-economic fabric, benefiting the 1% at the expense of the wider society.

Furthermore, populism, as discussed in "Silent Echoes", often champions policies that inadvertently serve the interests of the financial elite, from tax cuts for the wealthy to deregulation that allows corporations more freedom, often at the expense of the working class and the environment. In this light, the rational appeal of populism often masks the long-term negative impacts it imposes on the 99%, further entrenching inequality and societal discord.

Understanding the rationality and impact of populism is essential for the 99% as they navigate through the intricate landscapes of contemporary political discourse. "Silent Echoes" encourages you to approach populist narratives with a discerning and critical mindset, unpacking the simplistic appeals to unveil the deeper, often detrimental implications and impacts that these narratives hold for society at large. Through this lens, the book equips its audience with the necessary analytical tools to dissect and counter the allure and dangers of populism, advocating for a more informed, rational, and equitable societal framework.

Following is a critical lens through which to view the impacts of populism by looking at the economic, humanitarian, and environmental outcomes in countries under populist control. By assessing real-world cases, you are better positioned to understand the tangible repercussions beyond the attractive, yet often misleading, populist rhetoric.

Economically speaking, the wealth gap in countries like Brazil under Jair Bolsonaro has widened. Despite promises of economic revitalization for all, policies have often favoured the wealthy elite with significant tax breaks and deregulation for large corporations. These measures have resulted in limited economic relief for the working class, exacerbating income inequality and financial insecurity among the masses.

From a humanitarian standpoint, the situation in Hungary under Viktor Orbán provides a stark example. Orbán's regime has been marked by a notable decline in human rights, with policies and rhetoric that marginalize refugees and minority groups, fostering an atmosphere of intolerance and discrimination. Social welfare programs have been cut, leaving the vulnerable without essential support, while democratic institutions have been systematically weakened.

In the realm of environmental policy, the United States during the Trump administration saw significant rollbacks of environmental protections. The administration withdrew from international environmental agreements like the Paris Accord, reduced restrictions on carbon emissions, and favoured fossil fuel industries, showing disregard for long-term environmental sustainability and global cooperative efforts to combat climate change.

The reader is encouraged to delve deeper into the implications and consequences of populist control by examining the real-life examples provided by these and other countries. By scrutinizing the economic, humanitarian, and environmental impacts observed, you can sift through populist promises and slogans to understand the reality of such governance. With this understanding, individuals can make informed decisions and advocate for policies and leadership that genuinely represent the needs and aspirations of the majority, pushing towards a world characterized by equity, compassion, and sustainability.

"Silent Echoes" acknowledges that an objective assessment of populism must consider counterarguments, addressing the merits and defences often put forward by advocates of populist movements and governments.

Supporters of populist leaders like Brazil's Jair Bolsonaro or Hungary's Viktor Orbán often point to their decisive governance styles, asserting that such leaders take firm stances and effectual actions, which can be crucial in times of national crisis. These leaders are seen as champions of national sovereignty, protecting the interests of their nations against global institutions that might seem detached or even exploitative.

In defense of economic policies under populism, proponents argue that tax cuts and deregulations are necessary to stimulate economic growth and incentivize business investments. They believe this approach fosters a favourable climate for job creation and innovation, leading to broader societal benefits. For instance, the economic policies under the Trump administration in the United States were lauded for achieving low unemployment rates and stock market growth before the COVID-19 pandemic.

Regarding humanitarian issues, defenders of populism argue that their leaders are merely responding to the desires of the majority, safeguarding cultural identity and national values from the perceived threats posed by immigration and globalization.

They claim that the tightening of social welfare policies is a prudent measure to prevent abuse and ensure that resources are allocated to those who contribute positively to society.

In terms of environmental policy, populists often argue for a balanced approach that considers the immediate economic needs of their citizens. Supporters might contend that stringent environmental regulations can hamper business and employment, advocating for a more gradual transition to sustainability that does not compromise the livelihoods of the current generation.

We recognise that these defences of populism resonate with significant portions of the population and that they should be critically but fairly engaged. By addressing these counterarguments head-on, the book encourages you to undertake a nuanced and balanced examination of populism, weighing its appeals against its risks and costs to arrive at a well-informed perspective. Through such careful consideration, "Silent Echoes" seeks to facilitate constructive dialogue and reflection on the path forward for societies grappling with the challenges and allure of populist movements.

An invitation is extended to you to thoughtfully scrutinize the repercussions of populist politics, especially when our interconnected world is faced with unprecedented challenges; climate change, AI emergence, and significant health crises like COVID-19.

In the critical domain of climate change, populist figures such as the administrations of Donald Trump in the United States and Jair Bolsonaro in Brazil, significant environmental policies and protections were either rolled back or neglected, leading to substantial environmental destruction and potentially long-term ecological impacts.

Under President Trump, the U.S. witnessed a series of regulatory rollbacks that weakened environmental protections. Key actions included the U.S. withdrawal from the Paris Climate Agreement, a global effort to combat climate change, and the reduction of national monuments' boundaries, such as Bears Ears and Grand Staircase-Escalante, which opened up these areas to mining and drilling. The administration also rolled back the Clean Power Plan, which aimed to reduce carbon emissions from power plants, and relaxed regulations on air and water pollution. These actions have not only contributed to increased greenhouse gas emissions but also put vulnerable ecosystems and species at risk. The long-term impacts could include exacerbated climate change, loss of biodiversity, and compromised public health due to pollution.

Similarly, under President Bolsonaro, Brazil saw a surge in environmental degradation, particularly in the Amazon rainforest, which is crucial for global climate regulation. His government weakened environmental agencies, leading to reduced enforcement of environmental laws. This emboldened illegal logging, mining, and land-clearing for agriculture in the Amazon, resulting in a significant increase in deforestation rates. The loss of forest cover not only threatens the rich biodiversity of the Amazon but also impacts indigenous communities and contributes to carbon emissions. If this trend continues, it could push the Amazon rainforest closer to a tipping point, turning it from a carbon sink to a carbon source and drastically affecting global climate patterns.

These policy directions under Trump and Bolsonaro have set back environmental conservation efforts significantly. Reversing this damage and mitigating future impacts will require concerted global efforts and a renewed commitment to environmental protection and sustainable development.

Moreover, the relationship between populist leaders and industries with significant environmental footprints, like the fossil fuel sector, is noteworthy. The propagation of climate change misinformation and the dismantling of vital environmental safeguards under populist leadership play into the hands of these industries. Such maneuvers ensure sustained profits for these sectors at the cost of environmental sustainability and public health, sidelining the imperative of long-term planning for a sustainable future.

The global COVID-19 pandemic further spotlighted the dangerous intersection of populism and conspiracy theories. A case in point is Brazil, where President Bolsonaro consistently downplayed the virus's severity, promoted unproven treatments, and expressed scepticism towards vaccines, resulting in one of the world's highest COVID-19 death rates. Comparatively, nations led by governments that respected and followed scientific advice, such as New Zealand under Prime Minister Jacinda Ardern, have been more successful in controlling the virus spread and minimizing fatalities.

AI, with its transformative potential, also raises critical ethical concerns, necessitating global collaboration to establish robust ethical standards and governance frameworks. However, populist regimes might opt for isolationist strategies, potentially leveraging AI for surveillance and control, often rationalized through conspiracy theories framing national security threats, which pose significant risks to global human rights and digital freedom.

Through the discerning lens provided, you are encouraged to acknowledge the harmful effects of conspiracy theories, often amplified by populist leaders, on global attempts to navigate shared challenges. This understanding is crucial for advocating informed, collaborative approaches to addressing these pressing threats. Engaging with this reflective narrative allows you to champion leadership that is committed to factual integrity, dismisses unfounded conspiracies, and promotes collective global well-being and advancement.

This is a nuanced yet crucial aspect of populist governance: the subtle serving of the elite 1%'s interests. Though populist leaders project themselves as advocates for the masses, a deeper analysis reveals a substantial alignment of their policies with the desires of the wealthy elite.

The often-championed tax cuts in populist regimes, marketed as catalysts for job growth and economic vitality, predominantly favour wealthy corporations and individuals. This approach results in a financial drain on public services essential for the majority, fostering a widening gap of income inequality and underfunding in crucial societal infrastructure.

This concept coined "trickle-down economics," popularized during the eras of Margaret Thatcher and Ronald Reagan, has faced considerable scrutiny and criticism over the decades. Time and empirical evidence have increasingly shown that the idea, which posits that benefits provided to the wealthy and businesses will eventually trickle down to the broader population, seldom manifests as effectively in reality. This economic theory, often characterized by tax cuts for the rich and deregulation for big businesses, has not consistently translated into widespread economic benefits or improvements in living standards for the general populace. Instead, it has often led to increased income inequality and wealth concentration at the top, challenging the foundational claims of trickle-down economics as a viable strategy for equitable economic growth.

In shining a light on the alignment between populist policies and the interests of the wealthy minority, "Silent Echoes" invites you to sift through populist rhetoric critically. Acknowledging this disconcerting alignment is foundational for comprehending the underlying motivations steering populist movements and the unseen beneficiaries lurking in the shadows. Armed with this understanding, the electorate is better positioned to advocate for leaders and policies genuinely aligned with the welfare and aspirations of the broader public.

The Dichotomy of Populism

The term "populism" has become a ubiquitous yet polarizing force. It's a term that carries a dual narrative; one of autocratic, often secretive machinations by elites, and another of a genuine, grassroots movement for societal good. Understanding the distinction between these two forms of populism is crucial for discerning the underlying motivations and potential impacts of populist movements.

Some key markers can help distinguish the two:
- Rhetoric: Populist leaders who promote equality, justice, and the common good, such as MLK, often use inclusive language and rhetoric, calling for unity and solidarity. Fascist-type populists, on the other hand, tend to use more divisive and exclusionary language, targeting specific groups and othering them.
- Policy: Equality-based populists tend to focus on policies that promote social and economic justice, like healthcare, education, and workers' rights. Fascist populists, on the other hand, tend to focus on policies that target out-groups, such as immigrants, minorities, or political dissidents.
- Tactics: Equality-based populists tend to use peaceful means of protest, such as marches, rallies, and boycotts. (Concerns arise regarding the restriction or outlawing of peaceful protests in countries with democratically elected governments). Fascist-type populists, on the other hand, often resort to more violent and coercive tactics, such as intimidation, harassment, and state repression.
- Leadership: Equality-based populists often rise from within the group they are advocating for, and use their position to empower others.

The silent whispers of Autocratic populism, often cloaked in nationalism and traditionalism, have emerged as a powerful tool for political elites to manipulate public sentiment and gain power. Notable examples include the rise of leaders like Putin, Trump and Erdogan and the influence of figures like Steve Bannon and the Koch brothers in American politics. These entities often utilise secretive strategies and extensive funding networks to push their agenda.

"Dark Money, The Hidden History of the Billionaires Behind the Rise of the Radical Right" is a book by investigative journalist Jane Mayer, published in 2016. The book focuses on the influence of a network of extremely wealthy conservative donors on American politics. The primary subjects are the Koch brothers, Charles and David Koch, who have been major funders of conservative causes and candidates. Mayer details how these billionaires have used their wealth to exert political influence, often through secretive means. Her book uncovers how they have funded think tanks, academic institutions, and political campaigns to advance their conservative, libertarian agenda. This includes efforts to influence policies on issues like climate change, healthcare reform, government regulation, and taxes.

The narrative also explores the historical context of this movement, tracing its origins back to the early 20th century. Mayer articulates how the Koch brothers and their network have been able to significantly impact American political discourse and policy, often at odds with mainstream public opinion.

The term "dark money" refers to the undisclosed funds that are funneled through nonprofit organizations to influence elections and policy, without the donors' identities being publicly disclosed. This has raised concerns about the transparency and fairness of the political process in the United States. Overall, "Dark Money" is a critical examination of the role of wealth in American politics, highlighting the challenges it poses to democratic principles and the transparency of political processes.

This demonstrates how elite-driven populism can erode democratic norms under the guise of public interest, pushing a covert agenda that benefits a select few. Jane Mayer details the extensive efforts of the Koch brothers, in opposing various initiatives of President Barack Obama, especially in the realms of healthcare reform, environmental policy and alternative energy sources. The Kochs, who have significant interests in fossil fuels through their conglomerate Koch Industries, have been key figures in orchestrating opposition to environmental regulations and climate change initiatives.

The Koch brothers have been known to support groups and movements that oppose climate change legislation and environmental regulations that could harm their business interests. This includes funding organizations and think tanks that promote climate change scepticism or oppose renewable energy policies (as referred to elsewhere in this book).

The Koch brothers have been instrumental in funding and supporting grassroots movements, most notably the Tea Party movement, which gained significant momentum during Obama's presidency. This movement was critical in rallying conservative opposition against Obama's policies, including healthcare reform and environmental regulations.

Their financial backing extended to influencing elections, particularly the 2014 midterm elections, where their support helped secure significant victories for the Republican Party. This shift in power in Congress created a more favourable political landscape for advancing conservative agendas feeding the elites' vested interests and obstructing Obama's policy initiatives that would have benefitted the 99%.

Leading up to the 2016 presidential election, the Koch Network continued its efforts to shape political outcomes. While they did not openly endorse Donald Trump, their groundwork in previous years and continued political funding played a role in shaping the conservative political environment. The Koch brothers' involvement in American politics, as detailed in Mayer's book, highlights the significant impact of private wealth on public policy and political discourse. Their actions demonstrate a strategic approach to influencing key political outcomes, leveraging their vast resources to shape policies in line with their business ideologies and interests at a significant cost to the 99%.

The alleged connections and funding from Putin's Russia to various European far-right leaders underscore how autocratic populism often thrives on undisclosed relationships and financial dependencies, fostering policies that may undermine democratic institutions and principles. The allegations of Russian funding and support for certain European far-right leaders, including Matteo Salvini of Italy's League party and connections to figures like Nigel Farage, have been the subject of various investigations and media reports.

In the case of Matteo Salvini, Italian prosecutors investigated allegations of illicit Russian funding for his far-right League party. These allegations arose from media reports about a meeting between Russian officials and Salvini's close aide, where they reportedly discussed a secret oil deal to funnel money to the League party. Salvini denied these allegations, and there was no evidence that such a transaction took place. The investigation was looking into the possible crime of "international corruption." Furthermore, Salvini has been known for his public admiration of

Vladimir Putin and has been seen wearing T-shirts praising the Russian President.

L'Espresso, an Italian publication, reported on alleged secret meetings and potential financial arrangements designed to support Salvini's party through a scheme involving a Russian company. This reporting suggested that the objective was to provide clandestine support to Salvini's political activities, particularly ahead of European elections. The exposé outlined various aspects of this alleged scheme, including trips and meetings between Salvini's associates and Russian figures.

The investigation was initially opened in 2019 and focused on allegations of international bribery, following media reports that Salvini's former adviser, Gianluca Savoini, had held talks in Moscow with Russian businessmen about a possible oil deal that could potentially funnel funds to the League. Both Savoini and Salvini denied these allegations. Despite the serious nature of the allegations, the case was dropped due to the inability to gather enough evidence to support the claims. The request was based on the lack of response from Moscow to the assistance requests submitted by the Italian judicial authority.

An Italian judge decided to drop the case involving Matteo Salvini, leader of the League party, concerning the allegations of receiving illicit party funding from Russia. This decision came after prosecutors in Milan requested the dismissal of the case due to insufficient evidence to pursue the investigation further.

This decision came while Salvini served as both the deputy prime minister and the transport minister in Italy, and he expressed his expectation of apologies and the intention to sue others over the affair. This case and its dismissal have been a subject of significant public and media attention, reflecting the complex interplay of international relations, political funding, and legal proceedings in cases involving high-profile political figures and alleged foreign interference.

The connections between various authoritarian leaders and influential political figures such as Jair Bolsonaro, Donald Trump, Steve Bannon, Nigel Farage, Viktor Orban, Matteo Salvini and others are multi-faceted and complex. These connections are not necessarily defined by direct coordination or financial ties, but rather by a confluence of ideological similarities and strategic alignments.

Stephen Kevin Bannon has been a significant figure in shaping the landscape of contemporary autocratic populism. His journey from a media executive and political strategist to a key player in the administration of U.S. President Donald Trump paints a picture of a man deeply entrenched in the ideologies that drive autocratic populism.

Bannon's tenure as executive chairman of Breitbart News marked a pivotal shift in the platform's editorial stance, turning it into a mouthpiece for far-right and alt-right ideologies. Under his leadership, Breitbart propagated nationalist, anti-immigrant, and often conspiracy-laden narratives, influencing a broad segment of the population.

The Alt-Right is defined as a diverse and controversial political movement characterized by a range of right-wing ideologies. Key features include nationalism, anti-globalism, anti-immigration sentiments, white identity advocacy, anti-establishment stance, opposition to feminism, and a significant online presence. It is not a homogeneous movement, with varying beliefs among its followers. The Alt-Right is criticized for promoting extremist views, at odds with mainstream conservatism.

As the chief executive officer of Trump's 2016 presidential campaign, Bannon was instrumental in crafting a populist message that resonated with disaffected voters. His role as Chief Strategist in the Trump administration underscored his influence in shaping policy and rhetoric, particularly around issues like immigration and economic nationalism.

Bannon's vision extended beyond the United States. His intention to become "the infrastructure, globally, for the global populist movement" is indicative of his broader strategy. It's documented that Steve Bannon supported various nationalist and right-wing movements in Europe to form a unified front of populist ideologies against established political systems (democracy). He intended to contribute to the global populist movement, extending beyond the United States, and to align nationalist forces in Europe. Bannon's influence reached several European countries, where he sought to bolster right-wing movements that shared common ideological ground. This strategic approach aimed to create a cohesive and powerful alliance of populist ideologies challenging traditional political establishments.

Bannon has expressed support for Matteo Salvini, the leader of Italy's League party. Salvini has been associated with right-wing and nationalist policies. Bannon has been linked to Nigel Farage, a prominent British politician and leader of the Brexit Party. Farage is known for his nationalist and anti-EU stance. Bannon and Farage share common ground in their opposition to the European Union. Bannon has shown support for Marine Le Pen, the leader of the National Rally party in France. Le Pen is known for her right-wing and anti-immigration policies. Bannon sees her as part of the broader populist movement. While not a direct target, Bannon has acknowledged Viktor Orban, the Prime

Minister of Hungary, as a leader who shares some ideological similarities. Orban is known for his nationalist and anti-immigrant policies.

These figures represent a selection of Bannon's targets and partners in Europe. His efforts were aimed at fostering collaboration among various nationalist and right-wing movements to strengthen the overall populist influence in European politics. His ability to connect with the grassroots while operating at the highest levels of power showcases his unique position in the populist movement.

Bannon's approach has not been without controversy. His involvement in projects like Cambridge Analytica and the "We Build the Wall" fundraising campaign, which led to his arrest on charges of fraud, underscores the often opaque and legally dubious methods employed in pursuit of his populist agenda.

The "We Build the Wall" fundraising campaign aimed to raise funds for a border wall between the U.S. and Mexico. Started in 2018, it sought $1 billion on GoFundMe but contributed only about $1.5 million to the $42 million total cost. Legal issues arose, leading to charges against leaders, including Brian Kolfage and Steve Bannon, for defrauding donors. Kolfage was accused of covertly taking more than $350,000 in funds for personal use. Some associated individuals pleaded guilty. The campaign faced allegations of funds being used inconsistently with public representations. The exact amount raised and construction progress are not explicitly mentioned, and the campaign ended with legal challenges and accusations of fraudulent activities.

While at Cambridge Analytica, the same firm involved in influencing the BREXIT vote, promoted by populist Nigel Farage,

Bannon reportedly directed the company to explore messaging strategies about Putin and Russian expansion in 2014. This included focus group discussions about Putin and questions about Russian expansion in Eastern Europe. Bannon's interest in this area highlights his strategic consideration of Putin's role and image concerning American politics.

"Devil's Bargain: Steve Bannon, Donald Trump, and the Storming of the Presidency," written by Joshua Green, is a comprehensive exploration of the partnership between Steve Bannon and Donald Trump that significantly influenced the 2016 U.S. presidential campaign. The book was published in 2017 and has been highly regarded for its in-depth analysis and behind-the-scenes insights.

Bannon played a crucial role in shaping Trump's campaign. His right-wing, nationalist themes strongly influenced Trump's political rhetoric and strategy. Beyond the campaign, Bannon's influence extended into Trump's administration. He was instrumental in shaping policies that echoed his nationalist and anti-establishment ideologies, such as the travel ban targeting Muslim-majority countries and a protectionist trade stance. The book delves into how Bannon's populist-nationalist ideas resonated with the white working-class, contributing to Trump's victory. Bannon viewed Trump as a vessel for his ideologies, which were central to the campaign's success.

"Devil's Bargain" highlights how the partnership between Trump and Bannon marked a significant shift in American politics. It details how their alliance tapped into and amplified right-wing sentiments, reshaping the political landscape. Critics and readers have noted the book's in-depth reporting and compelling narrative style. It's been described as a cautionary tale with a deep exploration of the political dynamics that led to Trump's presidency. "Devil's Bargain" is not just a political biography but also a critical analysis of the forces and personalities that shaped one of the most unexpected outcomes in recent American political history that continues to reverberate in the crucial leadup to the 2024 US Elections. It's a valuable read for anyone looking to understand the dynamics of the 2016 U.S. presidential election and the rise of the alt-right movement.

Bannon's strategies, while distinct, complement the covert operations of figures like the Koch brothers. Where the Kochs operate through funding and influence from the shadows, Bannon takes a more public-facing approach, using media and direct political involvement to push the populist agenda. Collectively, these approaches have significantly contributed to the rise of autocratic populism by undermining democratic norms and promoting nationalist, often divisive policies.

Steve Bannon's career epitomizes the blend of media savvy, political strategy, and nationalist ideology that characterizes modern autocratic populism. His efforts, both in the U.S. and globally, have significantly impacted the rise of populist movements, challenging traditional democratic processes and institutions. Understanding Bannon's role provides a clearer picture of the mechanisms driving the current wave of autocratic populism.

Here's a breakdown of the key factors linking these leaders:

Ideological Similarities
Many of these leaders share a common ideological platform characterized by nationalism, populism, and in some cases, traditionalism. This ideological alignment results in similar approaches to governance and public policy, particularly in areas like immigration, national sovereignty, and economic protectionism.

Global Political Climate
The rise of these leaders can be seen as a reaction to global trends, including growing public distrust in traditional political institutions, economic uncertainties, and societal changes. This has led to a global environment where authoritarian and populist rhetoric resonates with significant segments of the population.

Indirect Influences
The role of misinformation campaigns and cyber operations, like Russia's interference in the 2016 U.S. presidential election, exemplifies indirect influences that shape public opinion and electoral outcomes. In this scenario, then-candidate Donald Trump's public invitation to Russia to target Hillary Clinton's emails added a layer of direct appeal to these otherwise indirect methods. Trump's call, which was framed as a request for Russia to uncover Clinton's emails, blurred the lines between indirect influence and more direct involvement. This incident, coupled with Trump's often ambiguous stance on such interferences and the subsequent responses of his administration, has deepened the complexities in understanding the nature of these influences in the global political sphere. This direct request by Trump, juxtaposed with the broader context of indirect influence, highlights the multifaceted nature of political interference and the

challenges in categorizing these actions within traditional frameworks of international relations and election integrity.

Tactics and Strategies
Common tactics used by these leaders include leveraging nationalistic sentiments, employing "law and order" rhetoric, and often using strongman or masculine imagery as a symbol of strength. They also tend to undermine critical institutions, including the media and judicial systems, and use propaganda to consolidate power.

Public Gestures and Symbolism
Actions such as anti-corruption campaigns, although they might not yield substantial results, serve to bolster the image of these leaders as reformers and protectors of the national interest. Such measures can be effective in sustaining support for authoritarian regimes, even in the absence of tangible progress.

Historical Context
The patterns observed in the behaviours and strategies of these leaders reflect historical trends in authoritarian governance. The similarities in their approaches suggest a broader historical pattern rather than a contemporary, coordinated strategy.

While there are ideological and strategic connections among these leaders, evidence of a coordinated, behind-the-scenes global effort is more nuanced. The rise of authoritarianism often reflects and leverages a combination of global political trends, national circumstances, and individual strategies rather than a singular, orchestrated effort.

In this context, the term "Ideological Similarities" should not be misconstrued as representing a benevolent or "for-good" ideology. As evidenced, these ideologies are often financially backed and propelled by certain elite groups. Their primary objective is not to serve the broader public interest, but rather to manipulate and exploit the majority, the 99%, for their own benefit, thereby safeguarding their vested interests. This stark reality underscores the fact that these ideological alignments, far from being altruistic, are strategically used to maintain and enhance the power and wealth of the elite at the expense of the general populace while dividing the populace.

In contrast, for-good populism arises naturally from authentic public dissatisfaction, unlike the discontent stoked by would-be autocrats. It seeks to rectify societal injustices and systemic flaws and is marked by its transparency and dedication to democratic principles.

Genuine populist movements are often grassroots, emerging from the collective dissatisfaction of ordinary people. These movements are transparent in their intentions and inclusive in their approach, aiming to create a more equitable society. Unlike autocratic populism, for-good populism thrives on transparency and accountability to its base. It is a movement for the people, by the people, and of the people, devoid of hidden agendas or clandestine funding.

What about Soros, I hear you ask! That is a very good point and so I carried out some in-depth research. This is what I have found.

George Soros is a billionaire philanthropist often targeted in conspiracy theories, particularly by right-wing and populist groups. The implication often is that Soros, like some figures in autocratic populism, uses his wealth to covertly influence political movements, which could be perceived as contradicting the grassroots, transparent nature of genuine populist movements.

It's true that George Soros, through his foundations, has funded various organizations and causes around the world, it's important to differentiate between philanthropic funding and the clandestine, manipulative funding often associated with autocratic populism. Soros's contributions are usually made through established channels and are a matter of public record, aligning with the principles of transparency. His funding often supports human rights, education, and democratic governance, which aligns with the ethos of for-good populism that seeks to empower and uplift communities.

Moreover, the core of for-good populism lies in its grassroots origin — it's driven by the collective will and needs of ordinary people, not just by the actions or contributions of a single individual, regardless of their financial influence. It's crucial to distinguish between the transparent support for democratic and societal causes and the secretive, self-serving manipulations of autocratic populism. In genuine populist movements, the power and direction come from the bottom up, reflecting the collective voices and interests of the people involved, rather than being imposed or orchestrated from the top down.

George Soros, through his Open Society Foundations, openly funds a wide range of initiatives globally, focusing on democracy, human rights, and social justice. This funding is a matter of public record and is done transparently. However, conspiracy theories often distort these activities, attributing hidden and malevolent motives without evidence. Soros has become a convenient scapegoat for various groups, often for actions or changes they oppose. These conspiracy theories typically lack credible evidence and often stem from or contribute to anti-Semitic tropes, given Soros's Jewish background.

A key feature of for-good populism is its transparency and accountability. Even when individuals or foundations like Soros's provide funding, the movements they support are typically open about their sources of funding and their objectives. This transparency is in stark contrast to the secretive nature often associated with autocratic populism and its funding. In assessing any external influence on populist movements, whether attributed to Soros or others, it's vital to critically evaluate the evidence. This involves considering the source of funding, the stated intentions of the funders, the alignment of the funding with the movement's goals, and the movement's own autonomy and grassroots support.

Understanding the role of disinformation in spreading conspiracy theories is crucial. Many claims about Soros are amplified by networks known for misinformation, and debunking these claims involves consulting reliable, independent sources for information.

While conspiracy theories about Soros are widespread, distinguishing between these and factual information about his philanthropic activities is essential. Genuine populist movements, despite receiving support from wealthy individuals or foundations, maintain their grassroots essence through transparency, accountability, and a strong connection to the communities they represent. It's crucial to rely on verified information and avoid unsubstantiated claims, by thorough, unbiased, fact-finding.

Autocratic populism serves the interests of a narrow elite and is characterized by policies that consolidate power and suppress dissent. For-good populism, on the other hand, seeks broad societal reform and greater public welfare. As shown, autocratic populism operates through secretive meetings and undemocratic tactics, as seen in the Koch brothers' approach. In contrast, for-good populism embraces open dialogue, democratic participation, and transparent decision-making. Autocratic populism often undermines democratic institutions and norms, while for-good populism seeks to strengthen them.

The distinction between autocratic and for-good populism is crucial in today's political discourse. Autocratic populism, driven by elites, poses a significant threat to democratic principles, often operating under a veil of secrecy and self-interest. In contrast, for-good populism emerges as a democratic response to societal grievances, characterized by transparency, grassroots support, and a commitment to the public good. Recognizing these differences is key to understanding and responding to the populist movements shaping our world.

Navigating the Globalization Paradox

In the swirling currents of global politics and economics, the concept of globalization has become a double-edged sword, wielded deftly by the elite to maintain their dominion while simultaneously being demonized as a threat to the general populace. This chapter seeks to dissect this complex paradox, highlighting how the elite has manipulated the narrative around globalization to their benefit, often at the expense of the 99%.

Globalization, in its essence, is the process of increasing interconnectedness and interdependence among countries, primarily driven by economic integration, technological advancements, and cultural exchange. Initially heralded as a harbinger of prosperity and a tool for bridging global divides.

The Panama Papers also showcased globalization's positive aspect; transparency. The investigation itself was a testament to global cooperation among journalists and analysts, made possible by the very fabric of globalization. It unveiled how increased transparency and global collaboration could challenge the entrenched systems of financial secrecy that the elite has long exploited.

The reaction of the elite to this newfound transparency is telling. Traditionally protected by financial and bureaucratic borders, they found themselves vulnerable to exposure in a world where national boundaries became less protective. This led to a defensive "crab crawl backward," a retreat to nationalism and protectionism by those who once championed globalization.

This retreat is often masked in rhetoric that claims globalization is detrimental to the masses, a narrative meticulously crafted to sway public opinion. It's a strategic diversion, steering the discourse away from the core issue; the exploitation of globalization by the elite for their enrichment. This narrative conveniently ignores the benefits globalization has brought in terms of economic growth, technological advancement, and cultural exchange.

The critique of globalization by the elite hinges on several points: it undermines national sovereignty, erodes cultural identity, and exacerbates economic inequality. However, these arguments are often selectively presented, ignoring the broader context. For instance, while globalization has indeed contributed to economic disparities, it has also lifted millions out of poverty and created unprecedented opportunities for many.

The elite's backlash against globalization also aligns with the rise of populist movements. Populism, with its simplistic and emotionally charged rhetoric, provides a convenient vehicle for the elite to push back against the forces of globalization. By blaming globalization for various societal woes, they deflect attention from the systemic inequalities and policy failures that they have perpetuated.

Moreover, the retreat from globalization isn't just about economics; it's about maintaining power. In a more integrated and transparent world, the traditional mechanisms of power and influence that elites have relied upon are less effective. By undermining globalization, they seek to reestablish the barriers that once insulated them from scrutiny and competition.

As a result, the discourse around globalization is often mired in controversy and skepticism, particularly when it comes to its impact on the broader population; the 99%. While criticisms of globalization focus on its role in exacerbating inequalities and serving elite interests, it's imperative to acknowledge the multifaceted benefits it has brought to the majority. We shed light on the numerous advantages of globalization for the 99%, underscoring how it has transformed lives, economies, and societies for the better.

One of the most significant benefits of globalization is its contribution to economic growth and poverty reduction. By fostering open trade and investment, globalization has enabled countries to tap into global markets, leading to economic expansion and job creation. For developing nations, access to larger markets has been crucial in driving growth and lifting millions out of poverty. The World Bank reports that globalization has been instrumental in reducing extreme poverty worldwide, with global poverty rates falling significantly over the past few decades.

Globalization has democratized access to information and technology. The rapid spread of the internet and telecommunications has connected the most remote areas to the rest of the world, breaking down information barriers. This accessibility has immense implications for education, health, and social awareness, enabling people to access knowledge, medical advancements, and global support networks.

The increased interconnectedness brought about by globalization has facilitated a rich exchange of cultures. This cultural osmosis has broadened perspectives, fostering greater tolerance and understanding among diverse populations. Exposure to different cultures through food, music, art, and literature has enriched societies, making them more inclusive and vibrant.

Globalization has played a crucial role in improving living standards. The diffusion of technologies and innovations, along with the integration of global supply chains, has led to more affordable goods and services. For the average consumer, this means access to a wider variety of products at lower costs, enhancing their quality of life and purchasing power.

Though globalization is often criticized for its environmental impact, it has also enabled a coordinated global response to environmental challenges. Issues like climate change and biodiversity loss require a collective approach, and globalization has facilitated international agreements and cooperation, such as the Paris Agreement, which are vital in addressing these global challenges.

Globalization has been pivotal in advancing healthcare and disease control. The sharing of medical research, global health monitoring, and rapid response to health crises have saved countless lives. The global fight against diseases like HIV/AIDS and the recent rapid development and distribution of COVID-19 vaccines are testaments to the benefits of a globally integrated healthcare approach.

Increased labour mobility is another advantage of globalization. Workers have more opportunities to seek employment abroad, leading to better job prospects, skill development, and remittances that support families back home. This mobility has been a key factor in improving livelihoods and reducing income disparities within and between countries.

Globalization, contrary to the rhetoric often espoused by the elite, has not been the primary culprit in the widespread job losses experienced by local employees. This narrative is a strategic oversimplification used by the elite to justify a retreat from globalization, masking the more complex factors at play.

The primary driver of job displacement in recent years has been technological advancement and automation. The rise of digital technologies, artificial intelligence, and robotics has revolutionized the way industries operate, leading to significant changes in the job market. Many roles, particularly those involving repetitive or manual tasks, have been automated, resulting in job losses in sectors ranging from manufacturing to administrative services.

Another significant factor is the evolution of the global economy towards more knowledge-based and service-oriented sectors. This shift demands a different set of skills and qualifications, often leaving behind workers trained in traditional industries. The lack of adequate retraining programs and support for transitioning to new job sectors has exacerbated the impact on employment.

Moreover, economic policies favouring deregulation and corporate interests over worker protection have also played a role. These policies often lead to precarious employment conditions, wage stagnation, and weakened labour rights, further impacting job security and quality.

While globalization has contributed to changes in the job market, such as the relocation of certain industries to countries with lower production costs, its role is often overstated. In reality, globalization has also created jobs, opened new markets, and fostered economic growth, which can lead to more employment opportunities in different sectors.

As demonstrated, the assertion that globalization is the primary cause of job losses is a narrative used by the elite to redirect attention from the actual factors, such as technological advancements and policy decisions. Understanding the real causes is essential for creating effective strategies to address job displacement and support the workforce.

While the general narrative suggests that the elite consistently benefit from the processes of globalization, there are specific drawbacks that this group faces in an increasingly interconnected world.

One of the significant drawbacks of globalization for the elite is the heightened transparency and accountability it demands. With the advent of global media, social networks, and the ease of information flow, the actions and decisions of the elite are scrutinized more than ever before. This exposure can lead to reputational risks, legal challenges, and a demand for greater corporate and personal responsibility.

Globalization has led to more coordinated international efforts to combat tax evasion and close loopholes. Initiatives like the Base Erosion and Profit Shifting (BEPS) project by the OECD aim to prevent strategies that allow the elite to shift profits to low-tax jurisdictions. This global focus on fair taxation poses a challenge to the elite who have traditionally benefited from more opaque and less regulated tax environments.

The interconnectedness of global markets means that the elite are more susceptible to economic downturns in regions far from their own. Their investments and assets are more exposed to global market volatility, and financial crises in one part of the world can rapidly affect their wealth in another.

Globalization has introduced new competitors and disrupted traditional industries where the elite have historically held significant interests. The rise of digital economies, tech startups, and innovative business models challenge the status quo, forcing the elite to adapt quickly or risk losing their competitive edge.

There is a growing global sentiment against perceived inequality and the concentration of wealth and power. This sentiment often translates into social movements, policy shifts towards wealth redistribution, and greater scrutiny of elite actions. The elite face a backlash that can manifest in stricter regulations, higher taxation, and a more critical public eye.

For the elite who have traditionally relied on national structures and cultural influences to maintain their status, globalization presents a challenge. The erosion of national boundaries and the rise of a more homogenized global culture diminish their ability to leverage traditional forms of influence and power.

The Brexit saga sheds light on the dilemmas posed by the Globalization Paradox, illustrating a dynamic interplay among elite influence, public opinion, and the rise of nationalist tendencies. The move towards Brexit can be seen as a reaction to the forces of globalization, underpinned by apprehensions about national sovereignty, cultural identity, and perceived economic challenges linked to the European Union's policies. Among these concerns might have been the apprehension over increased financial transparency and the imposition of stringent checks and balances on financial operations. Given the UK's reliance on its financial sector, there was a reluctance to commit to greater transparency and regulatory scrutiny. This hesitation has been interpreted by some as the upper echelon safeguarding their interests while cloaking their motives in the rhetoric of 'national sovereignty' and similar themes. Additionally, Brexit was significantly shaped by political leaders who steered public discourse, capitalizing on nationalist emotions and simplifying intricate issues, such as the economic ramifications of detaching from the EU. This approach played a crucial role in shaping the narrative and direction of the Brexit movement.

This campaign strategy, focusing on emotions and misinformation, successfully swayed public opinion but also overlooked the practical and economic complexities of detaching from the EU. The post-Brexit period revealed these overlooked issues, such as economic challenges, trade complications, and internal divisions within the UK. Brexit illustrates the critical need for informed and nuanced public discourse in decision-making processes, especially when balancing national interests with global interconnectedness. It underscores the importance of critical thinking, transparency, and accountability in understanding and navigating the implications of globalization.

In conclusion, the elite 1%'s promotion of nationalism, presented as beneficial for the 99%, is a calculated form of gaslighting, employing media manipulation, political rhetoric, and social media influence to advocate for a retreat from globalization. This narrative, while appearing to champion the interests of the masses, actually serves to safeguard the elite's wealth and power, leaving the broader populace vulnerable to economic and social challenges. Meanwhile, globalization, presents its own challenges to this group, demanding increased transparency and adaptation to shifting global dynamics. Despite its complexities, globalization's positive impact on the vast majority is clear, contributing to economic growth, cultural exchange, and overall global advancement. It is vital for society to navigate these narratives with critical understanding, ensuring equitable benefits and a fair, inclusive global community.

Brexiting the Narrative

The Cambridge Analytica scandal, a significant global controversy, involved the unauthorized harvesting of personal data from millions of Facebook users. This data, initially collected for academic purposes, was later exploited by Cambridge Analytica to create psychographic profiles. These profiles were crucial in several political campaigns, including Ted Cruz's presidential campaign and Donald Trump's 2016 presidential victory. The scandal also had implications for the Brexit referendum, as Cambridge Analytica was implicated in the "Vote Leave" campaign. The firm's tactics, which included sophisticated data analysis and targeted advertising, were used to influence voter behaviour and sway public opinion towards leaving the European Union.

In Kenya, Cambridge Analytica was reportedly involved in both the 2013 and 2017 presidential elections, working for President Uhuru Kenyatta's campaigns. Their involvement raised concerns, particularly regarding the potential of their tactics to inflame ethnic tensions in a country where politics is already deeply divided along these lines.

The firm was also hired for the 2015 Nigerian presidential election, reportedly by an opposition party. The tactics allegedly used in this campaign were controversial, including the use of a campaign video that emphasized the risk of violence and extremism, seemingly aimed at dissuading people from voting for the incumbent.

Furthermore, in the Caribbean, Cambridge Analytica's parent company, SCL Group, had a history of engagement in various political campaigns. Their operations in these regions have been less publicly documented but are believed to involve similar data-driven and potentially manipulative campaign strategies.

The activities of Cambridge Analytica in these countries have been a subject of considerable debate and criticism, particularly regarding the ethical implications of their methods and the broader impact on the democratic processes within these nations.

These scandals brought to the forefront critical issues related to data privacy, the ethical use of personal information, and the significant impact of targeted advertising in political campaigns. It sparked worldwide debates and legal investigations into data protection practices, leading to increased scrutiny of social media platforms and data analytics firms regarding user privacy and consent. The fallout from the scandal was profound, not only for Cambridge Analytica, which faced backlash, legal challenges, and financial difficulties leading to its closure in May 2018, but also for the broader digital and political landscape. It highlighted the vulnerabilities in data privacy and the need for stricter regulations in digital advertising and political campaigning, especially in the context of influential political events like the Brexit referendum and U.S. presidential elections. The case underscored the need for robust legal frameworks to ensure fair political practices and protect personal data in a rapidly evolving digital world.

Here we explore the controversial involvement of Facebook and Cambridge Analytica in the Brexit referendum, highlighting how digital platforms and data analytics were manipulated to influence public opinion and gaslight the populace. We delve into the methodologies used, the ethical and legal implications, and the profound impact on democratic processes.

The Brexit referendum, held on June 23, 2016, was a watershed moment in modern British history. While the decision to leave the European Union was influenced by various factors, the role of digital campaigning, particularly the activities of Cambridge Analytica and its use of Facebook data, has come under intense scrutiny. Here we examine how these entities used sophisticated data analytics and social media strategies to sway public opinion towards a pro-Brexit stance.

Cambridge Analytica, a political consulting firm, gained notoriety for its data-driven approach to political campaigning. The company claimed to influence voter behaviour through targeted messaging based on psychological profiling. Facebook, a central platform in digital communications, was utilized as a conduit for these targeted campaigns.

The core of Cambridge Analytica's strategy involved harvesting data from millions of Facebook users without their explicit consent. This was achieved through a personality quiz app that not only gathered data from the users who took the quiz but also from their Facebook friends, exponentially increasing the data pool. This data included personal information, likes, preferences, and other metrics that were used to build detailed psychological profiles of users.

Leveraging the acquired data, Cambridge Analytica engaged in microtargeting, where content was tailored to resonate with the fears, preferences, and beliefs of specific user groups or individual citizens. This content ranged from political ads to misleading or false information, designed to exploit emotional triggers and sway opinions towards leaving the EU. Microtargeting allowed for the dissemination of hyper-specific messages that would have the greatest impact on an individual's voting decision.

The campaign's tactics included gaslighting, a form of psychological manipulation where false information is presented to make individuals doubt their understanding of events. This was evident in the spread of exaggerated claims about the EU, such as the infamous "£350 million a week to the NHS" bus advertisement, which was later discredited.

Facebook's algorithms, which prioritize content that engages users, facilitated the creation of echo chambers. These are environments where a user only encounters information or opinions that reflect and reinforce their own. This echo-chamber effect amplified the impact of targeted misinformation, reinforcing pro-Brexit sentiment among certain user groups.

The use of personal data without consent and the dissemination of misleading information raised serious ethical and legal questions. It sparked a debate about privacy rights, the ethical responsibilities of tech companies, and the need for regulatory oversight in digital campaigning.

The involvement of Cambridge Analytica and Facebook in the Brexit campaign highlighted vulnerabilities in democratic processes in the digital age. The ability to manipulate public opinion using data-driven tactics without transparency or accountability poses a threat to the integrity of democratic elections and referenda.

The narrative surrounding Brexit, is a tapestry of complex socio-political and economic threads, each contributing to the intricate pattern of contemporary British society and its place in the global community. Far from being a singular event, Brexit represents a pivotal moment in modern history, marked by its far-reaching implications, both anticipated and unforeseen.

The roots of Brexit stretch back to long-standing debates over British sovereignty, economic autonomy, and the nation's role in the European Union. The referendum campaign itself was a battleground of contrasting ideologies, with the 'Leave' camp emphasizing national sovereignty and control over immigration, and the 'Remain' camp highlighting the economic benefits of EU membership and the risks associated with leaving. The rhetoric was charged with emotion, tapping into deeper sentiments about identity, independence, and nostalgia for a past era of perceived British prominence.

The referendum's outcome, a narrow victory for Leave, sent shockwaves not only through Britain but across the world. The immediate aftermath was marked by political turmoil, economic uncertainty, and a deeply polarized society. The value of the British pound plummeted, and forecasts predicted significant economic downturns. Politically, the country saw resignations and leadership contests, reflecting the unanticipated consequences of the vote and the unpreparedness of both camps for the result.

Negotiating the terms of departure proved to be a Herculean task, fraught with challenges and setbacks. Complex discussions around trade agreements, citizen rights, financial obligations, and the particularly thorny issue of the Northern Ireland border dominated the discourse. The protracted negotiations highlighted the complexities of untangling decades of political and economic integration, as well as the challenges of reaching a consensus within a divided British Parliament and populace.

Economically, the immediate effects of Brexit are marked by uncertainty and instability. Investment slowed, and some businesses relocated their operations out of the UK. However, the full economic impact of Brexit remains a subject of debate and speculation. Proponents argue that it grants the UK freedom to negotiate its own trade deals and regulations, potentially opening new economic opportunities. Critics, however, point to the loss of unfettered access to the EU's single market and customs union, which had provided significant trade benefits.

The Office for Budget Responsibility (OBR) in its March 2023 Economic and Fiscal Outlook reported that the post-Brexit trading relationship with the EU is expected to reduce long-run UK productivity by 4% relative to remaining in the EU, mainly due to increased non-tariff barriers. Additionally, both UK exports and imports are expected to be about 15% lower in the long run. The OBR also notes that new trade deals with non-EU countries are not anticipated to significantly impact the UK's economy.

According to a report by the European Central Bank (ECB), UK goods trading volumes with the EU fell significantly post-Brexit, with exports and imports remaining below pre-pandemic levels until early 2022. The post-pandemic recovery in UK trade has also lagged behind other advanced economies, with UK exports around 10% below pre-pandemic levels by the end of 2021. Empirical evidence suggests a reduction in UK-EU trade in both directions, ranging from around 10% to 25%. Additionally, the ECB reports that Brexit's initial impact on UK goods exports has been more severe than expected, and the end of free movement for EU citizens has contributed to labour shortages, particularly in lower-skilled sectors.

The Office for National Statistics (ONS) has observed that nearly a quarter of trading businesses reported an increase in the prices of goods or services bought in November 2023 compared to the previous month, indicating inflationary pressures. Almost a quarter of trading businesses also reported a decrease in their turnover in November 2023. Looking ahead to January 2024, more than a quarter of trading businesses expect their turnover to decrease, which indicates concerns about future financial performance. Furthermore, almost two-thirds of businesses reported some form of concern for their business when looking ahead to January 2024.

These findings collectively illustrate the economic challenges faced by the UK post-Brexit, including reduced trade with the EU, lower productivity, increased inflationary pressures, and business uncertainties. The legal and geopolitical complexities, especially regarding the Northern Ireland Protocol and the UK's global influence, remain significant in the post-Brexit landscape.

Beyond economics, Brexit has had profound social and cultural implications. It has prompted a reexamination of British identity, with questions about what it means to be British in the post-Brexit era. The issue has also exacerbated divisions, not just between Leave and Remain supporters, but also within the constituent nations of the United Kingdom, fueling discussions about Scottish independence and the future of Northern Ireland.

On the international front, Brexit has necessitated a redefinition of Britain's role in the world. The UK faces the task of forging new relationships and trade agreements while maintaining its influence in international affairs. Brexit has also had implications for the EU, challenging its unity and prompting reflections on its own future direction.

As the UK navigates its post-Brexit reality, it faces the dual challenge of healing a divided society and establishing a new place in the global order. The long-term success of Brexit will depend on how the UK addresses these internal divisions and repositions itself economically, politically, and culturally. It requires a balanced approach that acknowledges the concerns of those who voted to leave while mitigating the risks and maximizing the opportunities of this new chapter in British history.

As is now clear, the decision of the United Kingdom to leave the European Union has led to a multitude of complex issues and financial challenges. These problems span across various sectors of the economy and have far-reaching implications, both domestically and internationally.

One of the immediate effects of Brexit was economic uncertainty, leading to reduced investor confidence and a slowdown in economic activities. This uncertainty primarily stemmed from unresolved questions about future trade relations and regulatory alignments with the EU. Studies have indicated that Brexit has harmed the UK's GDP growth, with predictions of continued slower growth in the short to medium term compared to a scenario where the UK remained in the EU.

Brexit has disrupted the UK's trade relations, particularly with its largest trading partner, the EU. The imposition of customs checks and new regulatory barriers has led to delays and increased costs for businesses. This has particularly impacted industries that rely on just-in-time supply chains, such as automotive and manufacturing. The new trade barriers have also affected the export sector, with many companies facing challenges in accessing the European market.

London, once known as one of the world's leading financial hubs, has faced challenges due to Brexit. The loss of passporting rights, which allowed financial firms based in the UK to operate freely across the EU, has led some businesses to relocate their operations to other EU countries. This shift could potentially reduce London's influence as a global financial centre and lead to a loss of jobs and tax revenues.

The UK has traditionally been one of the largest recipients of direct foreign investments (FDI) in Europe. However, Brexit uncertainty has made the country a less attractive destination for foreign investors. Concerns over future trade agreements and market access have led to a decline in FDI inflows, which are crucial for job creation and economic growth.

Brexit has also exacerbated regional economic disparities within the UK. Regions that were heavily dependent on EU funding, or on sectors like manufacturing and agriculture that benefitted from EU membership, are particularly vulnerable to the economic consequences of Brexit.

The UK government's public finances have been affected by Brexit. The economic slowdown has led to lower tax revenues, while at the same time, the government has had to increase spending to manage the transition and support affected sectors. This has implications for the UK's fiscal deficit and public debt levels.

As has been covered, the end of free movement between the UK and the EU has led to labour market challenges. Industries such as agriculture, healthcare, and hospitality, which relied heavily on EU workers, have faced staff shortages. The skills gap, particularly in sectors requiring specialized skills, has become more pronounced, impacting productivity and operational capacity.

Brexit has necessitated a massive overhaul of the legal and regulatory framework in the UK. Adapting to new trade laws, developing independent regulatory standards, and establishing new international agreements are complex and resource-intensive processes.

Finally, there is long-term uncertainty regarding the UK's economic trajectory post-Brexit. Questions remain about the country's ability to establish favourable trade deals outside the EU, the impact on its global influence, and how it will navigate the challenges of an increasingly competitive and interconnected global economy.

In conclusion, the Brexit referendum serves as a stark example of the intricate interplay between political decision-making and digital technology's influence. While Brexit was initially championed as a path to regain economic sovereignty, its actual implementation has led to a myriad of economic challenges for the UK. These range from currency devaluation and trade disruptions to uncertainties in the financial sector and strains on public finances, all contributing to a complex and evolving economic scenario. It's important to recognize that assessments and investigations into these events (Cambridge Analytica/Facebook) are ongoing, and new revelations may further clarify the extent of their roles and impacts on the Brexit outcome.

Romanticizing the Roar

The fossil fuel industry, long the bedrock of global energy supply, faces a paradox in the era of climate change. While the need for a transition to renewable energy becomes increasingly urgent, the industry and its proponents assert that such a transition is economically untenable. This narrative, deeply ingrained in public and political discourse, is a strategic maneuver to maintain the status quo. It's essential to understand that the real resistance to change stems not from economic impracticality for the wider public but from the vested interests of the fossil fuel conglomerates and their elite beneficiaries.

The core of the industry's reluctance to embrace renewable energy lies in its vast investments in fossil fuels. These investments are not just in physical infrastructure but also in long-term contracts, exploration rights, and political lobbying. Transitioning to renewables implies not just the creation of new investment streams but also the devaluation of existing assets – a phenomenon known as 'stranded assets.' For the industry, it's a battle to protect these investments, even at the cost of the environment and public well-being.

Contrary to industry narratives, the true cost of fossil fuels extends beyond immediate financial metrics. It encompasses environmental degradation, public health crises, and the looming expense of climate change mitigation. These hidden costs are borne by societies worldwide, often impacting the most vulnerable populations. The industry, however, has been adept at deflecting these costs, avoiding full responsibility for the environmental and health impacts of its operations.

The fossil fuel industry and its elite supporters have mastered the art of spreading FUD (Fear, Uncertainty, and Doubt), about renewable energy. By emphasizing the supposed economic hardships of transitioning to renewables, they have created a narrative where fossil fuels appear as the only viable economic option. This narrative cleverly shifts the focus from the long-term benefits of renewables to short-term economic challenges (that only impact their industry), masking the potential of new industries and job creation opportunities inherent in renewable energy sectors.

Contrary to the FUD narrative, transitioning to renewable energy presents significant economic opportunities. New industries in solar, wind, and other renewable sectors offer avenues for investment, innovation, and employment. History shows that economic transformations, while disruptive, can lead to new avenues of wealth and prosperity. The transition to renewable energy is not a zero-sum game; it's an opportunity for economic diversification and sustainable growth.

The resistance to renewable energy transition is not just about economic loss but also about a shift in power dynamics. The fossil fuel industry and its associated elite have long wielded significant influence over global energy policies and economies. Transitioning to a more decentralized and diverse energy landscape threatens this entrenched power structure. It opens the door to new players, reduces dependency on traditional energy sources, and potentially redistributes economic power more equitably.

The cost of not transitioning to renewables is far greater for the global population than for the elite. The adverse effects of climate change; extreme weather events, food insecurity, health risks; disproportionately impact the 99%. The narrative of unaffordability, pushed by the fossil fuel industry, neglects the long-term societal costs of continued reliance on fossil fuels.

The path to a renewable energy future is not only viable but necessary. It requires dismantling the myths propagated by the fossil fuel industry and its elite supporters. Public awareness and education are crucial in countering misinformation. Governments, civil society, and the international community must collaborate to create policies that facilitate this transition, prioritising long-term sustainability and equity over short-term profits of the few. The shift to renewable energy is not a burden but an opportunity, an opportunity for economic innovation, environmental restoration, and a more equitable distribution of resources. It's time to move beyond the FUD and embrace the potential of a renewable future.

The fossil fuel industry, facing existential threats from the global shift towards clean energy, has engaged in a sophisticated campaign to convince the public of a fundamental untruth; that transitioning to clean energy is economically unfeasible. This narrative serves to protect their interests by stalling or reversing progress towards renewable energy. The methods employed are multifaceted, combining public relations strategies, political influence, and manipulation of information.

The industry has invested heavily in public relations campaigns to frame fossil fuels as indispensable to economic growth and stability. These campaigns often highlight the immediate costs of transitioning to clean energy while downplaying or ignoring the long-term economic and environmental benefits. By focusing on potential job losses in the fossil fuel sector and the upfront costs of renewable technologies, they create a narrative that renewable energy is a luxury rather than a necessity.

One of the most potent tools in the fossil fuel industry's arsenal is political lobbying. By making substantial campaign contributions to sympathetic politicians and political parties, they gain significant influence over energy policies. This influence is used to advocate for subsidies for fossil fuels, oppose environmental regulations, and maintain the status quo. Politicians, swayed by these contributions, often echo the industry's talking points, further amplifying the narrative against the affordability of clean energy.

The industry has borrowed tactics from the tobacco industry's playbook, deliberately sowing doubt about the science of climate change and the efficacy of renewable energy. By funding think tanks and pseudo-scientific research, they've created a veneer of legitimacy to climate change denialism. This strategy muddies the public discourse and creates an environment where the necessity of transitioning to clean energy is questioned.

Control over media narratives has been a key strategy. The industry often utilizes its connections and financial clout to influence how energy issues are reported in the media. This influence ranges from sponsoring content that is favourable to fossil fuels to having industry pundits and experts dominate the discourse in media platforms, thereby shaping public opinion in their favour.

In regions heavily reliant on fossil fuels for employment, the industry has played on economic fears, suggesting that moving away from fossil fuels would result in massive job losses and economic downturns. This exploitation of genuine concerns effectively turns local communities into vocal opponents of clean energy initiatives, despite the potential for new job creation in the renewable sector.

The industry has been accused of misleading the public on the comparative costs of fossil fuels and renewables. By highlighting the dropping costs of fossil fuels (often without accounting for subsidies) and overestimating the costs of renewables, they create a distorted economic comparison in the public mind.

By lobbying for regulatory frameworks that favour fossil fuels, the industry creates an uneven playing field. This includes pushing for regulations and tariffs that make renewable energy more expensive or less accessible, reinforcing the notion that clean energy is not economically viable for the average consumer.

The fossil fuel industry, often perceived as a powerhouse of self-sustained profitability, is significantly bolstered by an unseen force: government subsidies. These subsidies, amounting to billions or even trillions of dollars annually, represent a hidden cost shouldered by the public, effectively skewing the energy market and obscuring the true costs of fossil fuels.

Globally, fossil fuel subsidies are staggering in their magnitude. According to the International Monetary Fund (IMF), these subsidies amounted to $5.2 trillion in 2017, accounting for 6.5% of global GDP. The United States, for example, has been providing an estimated $20 billion in direct subsidies to the fossil fuel industry each year, with additional indirect subsidies potentially raising that figure much higher.

Subsidies take various forms, often hidden in tax breaks, incentives, and direct funding. Tax breaks such as the Intangible Drilling Costs deduction allow U.S. oil producers to write off a substantial portion of their drilling expenses. Additionally, the Percentage Depletion allowance enables them to deduct a percentage of the oil well's gross income from their taxable income, regardless of the well's actual value.

These subsidies distort energy market dynamics, giving fossil fuels an unfair advantage over renewables. By artificially lowering the cost of oil, gas, and coal, they make these sources seem more economically attractive than they actually are. This market distortion hampers the growth of renewable energy sectors by making them appear less competitive in comparison.

Beyond direct financial costs, subsidies indirectly contribute to environmental and health detriments. The continued support for fossil fuels encourages higher carbon emissions, exacerbating climate change and air pollution. The World Health Organization estimates that air pollution causes about 7 million premature deaths annually. The economic cost of these health impacts, often unaccounted for in subsidy calculations, adds billions to the indirect subsidy tally.

The massive financial resources directed towards fossil fuel subsidies represent significant lost opportunity costs. These funds could be invested in renewable energy development, healthcare, education, or infrastructure. For instance, reallocating just a fraction of these subsidies towards renewable energy could significantly expedite the transition to a cleaner energy future.

Despite growing awareness, reducing fossil fuel subsidies has been met with resistance. The industry, deeply entrenched in the political and economic fabric of many countries, wields significant influence. Any attempts to cut subsidies often face political pushback, fueled by industry lobbying and the potential impact on jobs in fossil fuel-dependent regions.

Globally, there have been commitments to phase out fossil fuel subsidies, such as the G20 pledge in 2009. However, progress has been slow and inconsistent. The lack of a unified global approach and the varying national interests of G20 countries have hindered substantial advancements in subsidy reforms.

The fossil fuel industry, facing the rise of clean energy alternatives, has deployed a potent tool in its arsenal: emotional manipulation. Central to this strategy is the romanticization of the

Internal Combustion Engine (ICE), glorifying its roar and power as symbols of freedom, tradition, and identity.

The sound of the ICE engine has been deeply ingrained in automotive culture, often associated with power, performance, and freedom. Advertisements, movies, and popular culture have long celebrated the roar of gasoline engines, embedding them as symbols of excitement and status. This emotional attachment has been strategically exploited by the fossil fuel industry to create a sense of nostalgia and resistance to electric vehicles (EVs), which are often quieter and perceived as less thrilling.

Automotive companies, in conjunction with oil industries, have launched marketing campaigns that emphasize the sensory experiences associated with ICE vehicles – the sound of the engine, the smell of gasoline, and the feel of power. These campaigns aim to evoke an emotional response, tapping into the collective nostalgia and identity associated with traditional cars.

A significant part of this emotional appeal is directed towards car enthusiasts, who often view ICE vehicles as more than just transportation – they are a passion, a hobby, and a symbol of heritage. By playing into this sentiment, the fossil fuel industry fosters a community that is deeply attached to traditional automotive culture and resistant to the adoption of EVs.

The industry has also perpetuated the myth that ICE vehicles are superior in performance to EVs. Despite the advancements in EV technology that offer comparable, if not superior, performance, the perception of ICE vehicles as more powerful persists, fueled by emotional narratives rather than factual evidence.

Another emotional tactic is the exploitation of 'range anxiety' – the fear that an EV will run out of power without access to a charging station. This fear is magnified in public discourse, overshadowing the advancements in EV battery life and the expanding infrastructure for charging stations.

By focusing on the emotional appeal of ICE vehicles, the industry distracts from the urgency of climate change and the environmental necessity of transitioning to cleaner energy. The romanticised narrative around ICE engines serves to downplay the environmental impact of fossil fuels and delay the adoption of more sustainable alternatives.

The phenomenon of "dealers' sabotage" refers to the reluctance of car dealerships to embrace electric vehicles (EVs), a trend rooted in the economic structure of the automotive industry. Traditional car dealerships derive a significant portion of their revenue from post-sale services and repairs, a business model heavily reliant on the maintenance needs of internal combustion engine (ICE) vehicles. These vehicles, with their complex engines and numerous moving parts, necessitate frequent maintenance (like oil changes and transmission repairs), ensuring a steady income stream for dealerships.

In contrast, EVs, characterized by fewer moving parts, require less maintenance, leading to a substantially reduced revenue from service and repairs for dealerships. This disparity has prompted some dealers to resist the shift towards EVs, occasionally resorting to spreading misinformation about their drawbacks, such as limited range, lengthy charging times, and high battery replacement costs, to deter customers. Additionally, dealerships often exhibit reluctance in stocking EVs, attributing it to lower customer demand or insufficient infrastructure, but this is usually a strategic move to continue promoting more profitable ICE vehicles.

The transition to selling EVs entails a substantial investment in training sales staff and service technicians and updating service infrastructure. Many dealerships, viewing the market shift towards EVs as uncertain or slow (even due to their FUD distribution), are hesitant to undertake these investments. This resistance restricts consumer choice and accessibility to EVs, potentially impeding the broader transition to cleaner transportation technologies vital for reducing greenhouse gas emissions and addressing climate change.

The geopolitical implications of the world's energy transition are indeed profound and far-reaching. As China aggressively invested in renewable energy technologies, positioning itself as a leader in this field, much of the rest of the world lagged behind, influenced by the entrenched interests of the fossil fuel industry. This dynamic has led to a significant shift in global economic power and influence.

While China was harnessing the potential of renewables, developing expertise, and securing a competitive edge in solar panels, wind turbines, and battery technology, other nations remained largely tethered to traditional energy sources. The delay in embracing renewable energy by these countries, clouded by the fossil fuel industry's influence and the allure of short-term economic gains, has resulted in a missed opportunity for leadership in the global renewable energy market.

Now, as the urgency of transitioning to sustainable energy becomes undeniable due to climate change, many countries find themselves playing catch-up. The wealth and opportunities that could have been garnered through early investment in renewables have, to a large extent, been ceded to China. This shift not only represents a lost economic opportunity for these nations but also has significant implications for global power dynamics.

Norway's success in adopting electric vehicles (EVs) stands as a prime example that EVs are not only practical but can also become a mainstream mode of transportation. However, the narrative often pushed by the fossil fuel industry misleadingly attributes Norway's success solely to its small size, overlooking the essential per-capita aspect of EV adoption. This argument downplays the broader applicability of Norway's model to other countries, regardless of size.

Norway's approach to EV adoption has been multifaceted and strategic. The Norwegian government has implemented a range of incentives to promote EVs, such as exemptions from heavy taxes and duties imposed on internal combustion engine vehicles, free parking in city centres, and the use of bus lanes to avoid traffic. These incentives significantly reduce the cost of owning an EV compared to a traditional gasoline or diesel car. Additionally, Norway has invested heavily in building a robust charging infrastructure, making it convenient for EV owners to charge their vehicles. This comprehensive approach has resulted in EVs comprising a significant portion of new car sales in Norway, a feat achievable not because of the country's size but due to deliberate policy and infrastructural support.

The argument that Norway's success is purely due to its small size is a form of gaslighting by the fossil fuel industry. It's a tactic to create doubt about the feasibility of EVs in larger countries. This viewpoint ignores the fact that EV adoption is a scalable solution, where strategies can be adjusted per capita and tailored to different countries' unique circumstances. Large countries can replicate Norway's success by adopting similar incentives, investing in charging infrastructure, and encouraging public awareness about the benefits of EVs.

Moreover, the transition to EVs is not just about vehicle size or population but also about political will, public acceptance, and the readiness to invest in the necessary infrastructure. Countries around the world, regardless of their size, can learn from Norway's example. They can implement policies that promote EVs, invest in renewable energy to power these vehicles, and educate the public about the environmental and economic benefits of transitioning away from fossil fuels.

Norway's success in EV adoption is a clear demonstration that with the right mix of policies, incentives, and infrastructure, the transition to electric vehicles is practical and feasible on a larger scale.

The Climate Deception

Since the 1970s, a deceptive iceberg of disinformation has been shaping public and political opinions on climate change. The core of this manipulation lies within the fossil fuel industry, with corporations like ExxonMobil leading the charge. This chapter uncovers the extensive history of Exxon's efforts to undermine climate science, methods used and its successful lobbying against climate action, juxtaposing its internal scientific accuracy with its public denial of climate change.

In the late 1970s, Exxon's scientists conducted climate projections that not only predicted future global warming trends with alarming accuracy but also pinpointed when human-caused climate change would become evident, later empirically proven to be right. Astonishingly, despite these internal revelations, Exxon publicly downplayed climate change's significance and lobbied against measures to combat it. This hypocrisy highlights a disturbing trend of deception, where corporations like ExxonMobil have used their influence to manipulate public opinion and hinder climate action, all while being fully aware of the impending crisis.

As the fossil fuel industry began to grasp the catastrophic consequences of their operations on the environment, a counter-narrative was initiated. Recognizing the financial and reputational risks, industry giants like ExxonMobil chose to deny, distort, or downplay the scientific evidence of climate change. This marked the beginning of a disinformation campaign designed to sow doubt and confusion about climate change, delaying regulatory action and maintaining profit margins.

To undermine the credibility of climate science, the fossil fuel industry invested heavily in disinformation campaigns. These campaigns funded think tanks (as articulated in the chapter "The Dichotomy of Populism", and further explored here) and individuals who denied or cast doubt on established scientific facts. By creating an environment where scepticism could thrive, the industry aimed to delay or prevent regulatory measures that could impact their profits.

The industry's subliminal messaging created a fear of loss among the public and policymakers. By suggesting that climate action would lead to economic hardships, the industry evoked fear and resistance to climate policies. Furthermore, subliminal association linked climate policies with notions of personal sacrifice, framing climate action as undesirable and burdensome.

The industry painted climate action as economically harmful, suggesting that efforts to address climate change would lead to job losses and financial instability. This tactic played on public fears of economic hardship, discouraging support for environmental measures and maintaining the dominance of fossil fuels in the energy landscape.

Evidence of the public's unconscious adoption of industry narratives could be observed in instances of widespread pushback against climate initiatives. From organized opposition to renewable energy projects to resistance to environmental regulations, the industry's subliminal messaging effectively mobilized public sentiment against climate action. This unintentional and seemingly deliberate advocacy for the fossil fuel industry's interests by the manipulated public, was a manifestation of the public's internalization of the deceptive narrative, highlighting the powerful impact of subliminal messaging on shaping public perception and behaviour in the realm of climate change.

Charles and David Koch, the owners of Koch Industries, have long played a pivotal role in shaping the discourse around climate change and environmental policy (as also articulated elsewhere in this book). Known for their control over one of the largest private companies in the United States, largely based on fossil fuels, the Koch brothers have used their immense wealth and influence to fund a widespread campaign against environmental regulations and climate change legislation.

The Kochs have hosted annual donor summits, and secretive gatherings at luxury resorts that bring together wealthy donors, influential politicians, and conservative activists. These summits are strategic platforms for formulating plans to funnel money into think tanks and advocacy groups that align with their interests, particularly those promoting climate change denial and opposing environmental regulations.

Their substantial funding of the American Legislative Exchange Council (ALEC) has been instrumental in drafting model legislation to roll back renewable energy standards and challenge Environmental Protection Agency (EPA) regulations. Additionally, David Koch's founding of Americans for Prosperity (AFP) marks a significant investment in political advocacy against climate legislation. AFP's activities, ranging from organizing rallies to funding political campaigns and creating ad campaigns, have been crucial in discrediting climate science and opposing environmental measures.

The Kochs' support for the Heartland Institute, a group aggressively denying climate science, further illustrates their commitment to shaping public opinion on environmental policies. The Heartland Institute's conferences and reports consistently question the validity of climate change, critiquing environmental policies and promoting scepticism about scientific consensus.

In academia, the Kochs have influenced research agendas through significant donations to universities, particularly in economics departments. Their funding often comes with conditions that promote free-market environmentalism, which opposes regulatory approaches to environmental issues. This influence extends to their extensive lobbying efforts in Washington, where they have spent millions to sway energy and environmental policy, including efforts to weaken the Clean Air Act and oppose international agreements like the Paris Climate Accord.

The impact of the Kochs extends to the media landscape as well, with funded campaigns that spread misinformation about climate change. These campaigns typically portray environmental regulations as detrimental to economic growth and personal freedoms, effectively swaying public opinion against environmental action.

The cumulative effect of the Koch brothers' actions has been profound, fostering a climate of denial and creating political obstacles to environmental protection. Their network, dubbed the 'Kochtopus,' exemplifies the significant impact private wealth can have on public policy. Their legacy is evident in the delayed responses to climate change, the weakening of environmental protections, and a deeply polarized debate on climate issues.

The activities of Charles and David Koch underscore the challenges in the fight against climate change posed by influential private interests. Their strategic funding and coordinated efforts have effectively undermined scientific consensus and delayed critical environmental action, highlighting the need for greater transparency and accountability in political funding and influence.

To be clear, the consensus among actively publishing climate scientists is overwhelmingly in favor of the idea that humans are causing global warming and climate change; NASA states that 97 percent of actively publishing climate scientists agree that humans are causing global warming and climate change. Multiple studies find between 90 to 100 percent of climate scientists agree that humans are causing global warming, with many studies converging on a 97 percent consensus. A survey of over 12,000 peer-reviewed climate science papers found a 97 percent consensus in the literature that humans are causing global warming.

While there may be a small percentage of scientists who hold dissenting views, the overwhelming majority supports the understanding that human activities contribute significantly to climate change.

The dissenting "scientists" are, in most cases, either not scientists, or scientists not qualified in Climate; like going to the urologist due to heart problems! Here are some of the "influencer" climate skeptics, in no specific order, including their funding sources, qualifications, and key claims:

1. William Happer:
    - Funding: William Happer has been associated with the CO2 Coalition, a group known for downplaying the effects of carbon dioxide. The CO2 Coalition receives funding from sources linked to the fossil fuel industry.
    - Qualifications: Happer is a physicist and professor emeritus at Princeton University.
    - Claims: Happer has expressed skepticism about the extent and impacts of climate change. He has argued

that increased carbon dioxide levels may be beneficial for plant growth.

2. Bjørn Lomborg:
   - Funding: Lomborg is associated with the Copenhagen Consensus Center, and some critics have raised concerns about its funding sources. According to desmog.com, New York-based hedge fund manager Paul Singer's charitable foundation gave $200,000 to Lomborg's Copenhagen Consensus Center (CCC) in 2013, latest US tax disclosures reveal. Singer, described as a "passionate defender of the 1%", has emerged as a major force in the Republican party in recent years
   - Qualifications: Lomborg is a political scientist and author.
   - Claims: Lomborg acknowledges human-induced climate change but advocates for cost-benefit analysis and prioritizing other global issues over immediate aggressive climate action.

3. Ivar Giaever:
   - Funding: Giaever is on the "Who we are" of the Heartland Institute. The Kochs' support the Heartland Institute, a group aggressively denying climate science.
   - Qualifications: Giaever is a Nobel laureate in physics.
   - Claims: Giaever has questioned the consensus on anthropogenic climate change and has made statements challenging the severity of its impacts.

4. Ian Plimer:
   - Funding: According to a columnist in The Age, Plimer earned over $400,000 (AUD) from several of these companies, and he has mining shares and options worth hundreds of thousands of Australian dollars. Plimer is currently the non-executive deputy chairman of KEFI

Minerals since 2006, independent non-executive director of Ivanhoe Australia Limited since 2007, chairman of TNT Mines Limited since 2010, non-executive director of Niuminco Group Limited (formerly DSF International Holdings Limited) since 2011, and non-executive director of Silver City Minerals Limited since 2011. He is the former non-executive director of CBH Resources Limited from 1998 to 2010, former non-executive director of Angel Mining plc from 2003 to 2005, former director of Kimberley Metals Limited from 2008 to 2009, former director of KBL Mining Limited from 2008 to 2009 and former director of Ormil Energy Limited from 2010 to 2011. He was appointed director of Roy Hill Holdings and Queensland Coal Investments in 2012.

- Qualifications: Plimer is a geologist.
- Claims: Plimer has challenged mainstream climate science, arguing that climate change is natural and not significantly influenced by human activities.

5. Claude Allègre:
- Funding: Claude Allègre is a French geochemist. While his funding sources are not explicitly documented, he initially supported climate science but later became a critic of certain aspects of climate change research.
- Qualifications: Allègre is a geochemist.
- Claims: Allègre has questioned aspects of climate change research and has expressed skepticism about the severity of human-induced climate change. In a 2010 petition, more than 500 French researchers asked Science Minister Valérie Pécresse to dismiss Allègre's book L'imposture climatique, claiming the book was "full of factual mistakes, distortions of data, and plain lies"

6. Roy Spencer:
- Funding: Roy Spencer is a meteorologist and principal research scientist at the University of Alabama in Huntsville. His funding sources are not explicitly documented.
- Qualifications: Spencer is a meteorologist. The major difference between meteorologists and climatologists is that meteorologists predict weather for the near term, while climatologists study past weather patterns to predict trends.
- Claims: Spencer is known for his skepticism regarding the extent of human influence on climate change and has challenged certain aspects of climate science.

7. Judith Curry:
- Funding: Judith Curry is a former professor and climatologist. After leaving academia, Curry shifted to running the Climate Forecast Applications Network, a climate-risk consulting company its clients include energy companies.
- Qualifications: Curry is a climatologist.
- Claims: Curry is known for her critiques of climate science and climate models. She has expressed skepticism about the level of certainty in climate predictions.

8. Nir Shaviv:
- Funding: Nir Shaviv is an astrophysicist. He is a regular speaker at the Heartland Institute's International Conference on Climate Chance (ICCC), and has been listed as an advisor to both the Committee for Constructive Tomorrow (CFACT), and the Global Warming Policy Foundation (GWPF), although he has

denied his affiliation with the former. Dr. Shaviv says that he is not funded by the oil industry or large corporations
- Qualifications: Shaviv is an astrophysicist.
- Claims: Although he is skeptical of man-made climate change, he stresses that there are a "dozen good reasons why we should strive to burn less fossil fuels." His two primary reasons are pollution and depletion. He is in favor of developing cheap energy alternatives such as wind and solar power

9. Jan Veizer:
- Funding: Veizer was also a speaker at the Heartland Institute's 2009 (an Institute largely funded by the Kocks), International Conference on Climate Change.
- Qualifications: Veizer is a geochemist.
- Claims: While acknowledging the influence of CO2 on climate, Veizer has questioned the dominant role attributed to human activities in climate change.

10. Richard Lindzen:
- Funding: Richard Lindzen is a professor emeritus at MIT. His funding sources are not explicitly documented. Analysis of Peabody Energy court documents showed that the fossil fuel company backed Lindzen. In the article in 1995, Ross Gelbspan reports Lindzen charged "oil and coal interests $2,500 a day for his consulting services; his 1991 trip to testify before a Senate committee was paid for by Western Fuels. A decade later Boston Globe columnist Alex Beam reported, based on an interview with Lindzen, that "he accepted $10,000 in expenses and expert witness fees from fossil- fuel types in the 1990s.
- Qualifications: Lindzen is an atmospheric physicist.

- Claims: Lindzen is known for his skepticism of the consensus on anthropogenic climate change and has challenged certain aspects of climate science.

11. John Christy:
    - Funding: John Christy is a climate scientist and professor. Christy is perhaps the most prominent of a group of climate science outsiders who had become insiders in the Trump era. He has gained a seat on the EPA's Science Advisory Board, and won a $1.5 million Department of Energy grant for his research into the contrarian notion that the Earth's climate is relatively insensitive to carbon emissions.
    - Qualifications: Christy is a climate scientist.
    - Claims: Christy has been involved in climate research and has expressed skepticism about certain climate models and the severity of climate change.

12. Sherwood B. Idso:
    - Funding: Sherwood B. Idso is a physicist and former research physicist. Idso narrated the video titled "The Greening of Planet Earth," which was funded by the Western Fuels Association and by the coal industry and produced by Idso's wife. The video promises that doubling the atmosphere's concentration of carbon dioxide will benefit agriculture. Idso also appeared in the video to discuss the supposed benefits of CO2!
    - Qualifications: Idso is a physicist.
    - Claims: Idso is known for his work on the physiological effects of increased carbon dioxide and has challenged the severity of climate change impacts.

13. Fred Singer:

- Funding: Fred Singer is a former space scientist and government scientific administrator, he runs the Science and Environmental Policy Project (SEPP). This phantom organisation was set up by APCO & Associates, the PR firm controlled by Philip Morris, to denigrate science itself and enlist other industries like oil, energy, coal, chemicals, etc, behind the tort-reform and anti-regulatory stance necessary for the cigarette business to survive at the same high profit level. Singer was the front of the organisation, but it also involved his wife Candace Crandall and her brother Robert Crandall (Brookings Institution). In a sworn affidavit, Dr. Singer also stated that he had undertaken consulting work on "perhaps a dozen or so" energy companies. This included work on behalf of oil companies, such as Exxon, Texaco, Arco, Shell, Sun, Unocal, the Electric Power Research Institute, Florida Power and the American Gas Association.
- Qualifications: Singer is an atmospheric physicist.
- Claims: Singer has been a prominent skeptic of the scientific consensus on climate change, challenging certain aspects of climate science.

Please note that these individuals have varying degrees of skepticism, and their views do not represent the majority consensus in climate science as shown above. It's essential to consider the broader scientific community's consensus on climate change, which strongly supports the understanding that human activities contribute significantly to global warming.

The divisive narrative crafted by the fossil fuel industry has had far-reaching consequences on the global response to climate change. By creating ideological camps and deepening societal divides, this narrative has hindered constructive dialogue and collaboration, posing significant challenges to the development of effective climate policies. The industry, represented by entities like ExxonMobil and the Koch brothers, has skillfully exploited these divisions to further entrench its position, delaying essential global efforts to address the climate crisis.

The deceptive practices employed by these powerful players and their hired "influencers", have left a profound impact, not only on environmental policy but also on the planet and society as a whole. As the reality of climate change becomes more apparent and its effects more tangible, the urgency to counter these misleading narratives grows. This battle against climate misinformation is not just about implementing policy changes; it requires a fundamental shift in public perception. Guided by scientific evidence, truth, and a resolute commitment to the planet's future, society must come together to hold these entities accountable and champion sustainable solutions. The fight against climate change demands a concerted effort from all sectors, emphasizing the critical need for truth and transparency in addressing one of the most pressing challenges of our time.

Between Truth & Illusion

We now delve deeply into the crucial distinction between authentic science and the pseudo-science embedded within conspiracy theories, a differentiation vital for anyone navigating the contemporary landscape of information, misinformation and disinformation. Fact and authentic science represents an unceasing pursuit of understanding, grounded in scepticism, scrutiny, and empirical evidence. Unlike the self-validating pseudo-science found in conspiracy theories, real science is characterized by an ongoing process of self-reflection and correction. For example, our evolving understanding of the universe, from geocentric to heliocentric models and now to an expanding universe, exemplifies science's readiness to adapt based on new data.

In contrast, pseudo-science, often seen in conspiracy theories, seeks self-validation and is driven by confirmation bias. It typically begins with a preconceived conclusion and scavenges selectively for evidence that supports this belief while dismissing counter-evidence without genuine consideration. For instance, despite comprehensive studies debunking any link between vaccines and autism, the conspiracy continues, fueled by selective data interpretation and dismissal of scientific consensus.

Pseudo-science often revels in the mysterious and secretive, suggesting the possession of elusive knowledge accessible only to an enlightened few, creating an illusion of exclusivity. Consider conspiracy theories about secret societies like the Illuminati, which rely on secretive, non-verifiable information, drawing people into a web of illusion without empirical foundation.

Ironically, the scientific community can view conspiracy theories as unconventional critiques, challenging prevailing assumptions and provoking further inquiry. True scientific endeavours welcome scepticism and critique, rooted in questioning, testing, and refining hypotheses and theories. Unlike conspiracy theories, science doesn't claim possession of absolute truth but offers the best explanations based on current evidence, amenable to revision with new data.

While conspiracy theories could theoretically prompt constructive scrutiny, in practice, they often confuse discourse rather than contribute substantively. For such critiques to be valuable, they must adhere to rigorous standards of evidence and logic that underpin scientific inquiry, a criterion most conspiracy theories fail to meet.

For those navigating through complex informational landscapes, the task is to balance healthy scepticism with intellectual rigour. Engaging with unconventional ideas is moderately beneficial; it can be a stimulating exercise that sharpens critical thinking skills. However, it is crucial to approach such ideas with a discerning, analytical mindset, evaluating their merit based on evidence, coherence, and logical consistency.

Thus, while conspiracy theories might appear as intriguing alternatives or critiques to established knowledge, they need to be assessed with the same analytical rigour as any scientific proposition. Only then can they be considered valuable contributions to the broader tapestry of human understanding. If they fail to meet these criteria, they should be recognized as distractive noise within the symphony of informational exchange.

In "Silent Echoes," we encourage cultivating an approach to information that is both open-minded and critically discerning, recognizing the importance of evidence-based thinking in distinguishing valid critiques from misleading conspiracy theories. Such intellectual resilience is indispensable in a world where information is abundant, but wisdom is often scarce.

Understanding the divergence between science and pseudo-science is not just an intellectual exercise but a practical toolkit for navigating a world saturated with information and misinformation. Whereas science illuminates the path of understanding with its rigorous approach, pseudo-science obfuscates and misleads. Recognizing these differences empowers you to engage with information critically and discerningly, fostering resilience against manipulation and deceit.

Now, we undertake a nuanced exploration of conspiracy theories, deeply woven into the socio-political fabric of society and wielding significant influence over perceptions and actions. The allure of these theories is broad, captivating various demographics irrespective of education level, and often serving the interests of the elite subtly and effectively.

Understanding the psychology behind conspiracy theories is foundational to our discussion. These theories provide comfort and a semblance of control to individuals feeling marginalized or powerless, offering them a narrative that seemingly explains their socioeconomic circumstances while attributing blame to specific entities or groups. However, as seen with Brexit, these simplistic explanations are deceptive, drawing attention away from the real, systemic issues that demand collective action for genuine change.

Conspiracy theories' susceptibility transcends education levels, intertwined with feelings of disenfranchisement, historical distrust in institutions, and the influence of one's immediate social environment. This complex susceptibility extends across various groups within society, demonstrating that education alone does not immunize against such beliefs. Conspiracy theories do not serve the broader interests of society. While they provide illusory comfort and straightforward answers to complex questions, they deepen divisions, erode trust in vital institutions, and hinder informed societal participation. Their disempowering nature benefits the elite, consolidating their power and influence unchallenged.

Effective debunking strategies emphasize promoting critical thinking, approaching conspiracy theory believers with empathy and respect, utilizing trusted community messengers, and providing alternative narratives that address core fears and concerns. This strategic and empathetic engagement aims to reclaim the public's agency, fostering a society resistant to divisive and unfounded narratives.

The psychological allure of conspiracy theories is potent, offering simplified explanations for complex societal issues and a semblance of control in a seemingly chaotic world. The elite often exploit this inclination, subtly disseminating theories that divert attention from their actions and maintain their status quo. These narratives, stigmatizing specific groups within society, tap into existing fears and prejudices, further serving elite interests.

Conspiracy theories provide a false sense of agency and autonomy, particularly appealing to those feeling disenfranchised. They attribute challenges and inequalities to specific enemies or shadowy groups, offering a clearer sense of purpose and direction. However, while they provide psychological comfort, they ultimately harm adherents by obstructing their understanding of true situations and systemic issues. Critical thinking and awareness are needed to discern truth from fiction, enabling society to challenge and question narratives, and reclaim psychological agency from subtle manipulations.

Conspiracy theories, while seemingly empowering, serve to distract and divide the public, benefiting the elite. They perpetuate misinformation, foster societal divisions, and erode trust in institutions crucial for social equity and justice. Engaging with these theories based on misinformation impedes effective societal negotiation and understanding. Recognizing and resisting these narratives is imperative for the public to reclaim agency and work towards an equitable society that addresses diverse needs and aspirations.

When conspiracy theorists and pseudo-scientists are challenged with facts, they frequently resort to attacking the messenger or the institution, a tactic known as ad hominem attacks. This approach deflects attention from their unsubstantiated claims by targeting the credibility, character, or affiliations of the person presenting the facts, rather than the substance of the argument itself. It's a common defense mechanism in pseudo-scientific circles, especially when their assertions lack empirical support.

For example, in the realm of climate change denial, prominent climate scientists like Michael E. Mann, who present evidence of human-caused climate change, often face personal attacks. These attacks typically come from political groups or industries with vested interests in denying climate change and aim to discredit the scientists' research by accusing them of manipulating data for personal gain. Similarly, in the context of vaccine misinformation, medical professionals and researchers who counter such misinformation frequently encounter personal attacks. Dr. Paul Offit, a pediatrician and vaccine expert, has been repeatedly targeted with accusations of being in the pocket of pharmaceutical companies in attempts to undermine his credibility and the scientific consensus on vaccine safety and efficacy.

During the COVID-19 pandemic, health experts like Dr. Anthony Fauci faced numerous attacks from conspiracy theorists. When presenting scientific data about the virus's spread and the efficacy of masks and social distancing, these experts often faced accusations of fear-mongering or having ulterior motives, rather than engaging with the scientific evidence they presented.

The rationale behind such attacks lies in several psychological and strategic factors. By attacking the individual or institution presenting facts, the focus shifts from the weaknesses of the argument to the character of the person making the argument, distracting audiences from the lack of empirical evidence supporting the pseudo-scientific claim. These attacks often appeal to emotions rather than reason, evoking a stronger response and rallying support among those already predisposed to believe the conspiracy theory or pseudo-scientific claim.

Casting doubt on the credibility of a scientist or institution can lead people to question the validity of their findings, even if the evidence is sound. This strategy is effective in an era where trust in institutions and experts is eroding. For conspiracy theorists and pseudo-scientists, portraying themselves as victims of a smear campaign by powerful entities reinforces their narrative of being lone truth-seekers persecuted by a corrupt establishment. Furthermore, these attacks can strengthen the bonds within a community of believers, fostering a sense of solidarity among group members.

Understanding this method of defense is crucial in countering misinformation. Recognizing ad hominem attacks for what they are (a tactic to divert attention from weak or nonexistent evidence) is a key step in maintaining the focus on the factual accuracy of claims and the integrity of scientific discourse.

The susceptibility to conspiracy theories, driven by disenfranchisement and feelings of powerlessness, transcends educational or demographic boundaries. It is shaped by the dominance of money in politics and policies favouring a wealthy minority, exacerbating inequality and eroding trust in political institutions. Political leaders, even from left-leaning parties, sometimes fail to balance diverse interests, resulting in policies that do not address the majority's needs. Some Governments are taking steps to create more equitable economic policies, enhance social welfare programs, improve political representation, and boost transparency in political funding to mitigate the influence of big money and ensure inclusive policies.

The scientific method extends beyond the confines of traditional science; it is a rigorous process designed to separate fact from myth, and truth from falsehood. This method, fundamental to scientific inquiry, is not exclusively confined to the laboratory or scientific research; it is a comprehensive framework that can be applied to various fields and aspects of life to discern accurate information and draw reliable conclusions.

At its core, the scientific method is a systematic approach to investigating phenomena, acquiring new knowledge, or correcting and integrating previous knowledge. It is based on empirical or measurable evidence subject to specific principles of reasoning. The method typically involves the following steps; making observations, forming a hypothesis, conducting experiments or gathering data, analyzing the results, and drawing conclusions. If the results consistently support the hypothesis, it gains credibility. If not, it is revised or discarded.

This method's strength lies in its reliance on empirical evidence and its iterative nature, allowing for continual testing and refinement of hypotheses. This approach ensures that conclusions are not based on preconceived notions or untested beliefs but are supported by observable and measurable evidence.

In separating fact from myth, the scientific method encourages scepticism and critical thinking. It demands that claims be scrutinized and tested and that conclusions be based on evidence rather than conjecture or hearsay. This process is invaluable not only in scientific research but also in everyday decision-making, where distinguishing between accurate information and misinformation is crucial.

For instance, in public health, the scientific method is used to evaluate the effectiveness and safety of medications and treatments. In environmental studies, it is applied to understand the impacts of human activities on the environment. Even in the social sciences, it plays a crucial role in examining social behaviours, political and societal trends.

Overall, the scientific method is a powerful tool for inquiry and understanding, promoting a disciplined approach to discerning the truth and challenging myths and misconceptions. Its application extends far beyond traditional science, serving as a fundamental guide in various domains for making informed, evidence-based decisions.

Authoritarian challengers exploit vulnerabilities and sow division, using disinformation, supporting populist movements, conducting cyber attacks, and exerting economic leverage to influence democratic nations. They exploit political and social fissures, weaken international alliances, and promote authoritarian ideals, especially where democracies struggle.

The tactics of authoritarian challengers can be seen as a form of pseudo-science or manipulation of information to serve specific political agendas. These tactics are stark examples of how truth can be distorted and illusion created, undermining the principles of scientific inquiry and informed decision-making.

For instance, the Russian interference in the 2016 U.S. Elections, involving a disinformation campaign, aligns with the pseudo-scientific manipulation of facts. It demonstrates how data and information can be twisted to create a narrative that serves particular interests, much like pseudo-science distorts evidence to fit preconceived conclusions.

The use of cyber warfare by authoritarian regimes, such as the Russian attacks on Ukraine, showcases a more direct form of manipulation, akin to how pseudo-science often employs technology to propagate misleading information.

In exploiting political and social fissures, as seen in Russia's support for separatist movements, and in promoting authoritarian ideals globally, as China does with its internet censorship model, these regimes create a facade of legitimacy and truth. This tactic mirrors how pseudo-science creates an illusion of credibility, often using complex jargon and false narratives to obscure the lack of empirical evidence.

Therefore, the actions of authoritarian challengers can be understood as real-world manifestations of the very principles that distinguish pseudo-science from genuine science. They exemplify how misinformation and distorted facts can lead to widespread misconceptions and misguided decisions, emphasizing the chapter's theme of navigating the delicate balance between truth and illusion in our contemporary world.

Corporations, even within the health field, have at times engaged in practices that aim to deceive customers or manipulate information to their advantage. However, such instances of corporate misconduct do not invalidate the scientific method; rather, they highlight the importance of applying this method rigorously and maintaining ethical standards in all scientific and corporate endeavors.

One real example of corporate deception is the case involving Purdue Pharma and the opioid crisis. Purdue Pharma, the maker of OxyContin, a powerful opioid painkiller, was accused of downplaying the risks of addiction associated with the drug while aggressively marketing it to doctors and patients. The company's misleading marketing practices contributed significantly to the opioid epidemic in the United States, leading to widespread addiction and numerous deaths. In 2020, Purdue Pharma pleaded guilty to federal criminal charges related to its aggressive and misleading marketing of OxyContin.

Another example is the tobacco industry's long history of misleading the public about the health risks of smoking. For decades, tobacco companies conducted campaigns to cast doubt on scientific evidence linking smoking to lung cancer and other diseases. They employed tactics like funding their own research to contradict independent studies and aggressively marketing their products despite knowing the health risks.

While there are examples of corporate misconduct that have misled the public and exploited scientific claims, these actions represent a deviation from, rather than a disqualification of, the scientific method. The continued application of rigorous, unbiased scientific inquiry remains a critical tool in discerning truth and safeguarding the public interest.

Instances of corporate misconduct, as seen with Purdue Pharma in the opioid crisis and tobacco companies downplaying smoking risks, cause significant harm to consumers. This issue becomes more severe when combined with pseudo-scientific narratives in areas like climate change, artificial intelligence (AI), and populism. The oil industry, for example, has been accused of promoting false research to minimize the perception of climate change, delaying crucial environmental action. In the field of AI, misinformation can lead to ill-informed policies affecting societal norms and job markets. Similarly, populist movements often exploit pseudo-scientific rhetoric, undermining democratic processes and civil liberties. These combined effects of corporate wrongdoing and pseudo-science highlight the need for informed public discourse and strong regulatory measures to protect civil liberties and ensure our species' long-term survival.

These instances demonstrate that corporate interests can occasionally result in unethical and potentially counter-existential practices, which sharply diverge from the principles upheld by the scientific method. Fundamental to the scientific method are transparency, peer review, and the ability to reproduce results, ensuring both the reliability and accuracy of scientific findings. However, when corporate entities place profit above these critical scientific principles, it not only undermines public trust but can also lead to significant harm.

These instances of corporate misconduct should not be seen as a failure of the scientific method itself. Instead, they underscore the need for stricter regulatory oversight, ethical corporate practices, and public awareness. They also highlight the importance of independent scientific research and inquiry, free from corporate influences, to ensure that the conclusions drawn are based on sound evidence and unbiased analysis.

In response to such challenges, there have been increasing calls for more stringent regulation of pharmaceutical marketing, better oversight of corporate-sponsored research, and greater transparency in the dissemination of scientific information. These measures are essential to uphold the integrity of scientific research and protect public health and well-being.

Democracies must strengthen cybersecurity, combat disinformation, maintain electoral integrity, and uphold values and international cooperation. Addressing internal challenges like economic inequality, political corruption, and social divisions reduces vulnerabilities authoritarian challengers exploit, maintaining robust, inclusive democracy resilient to divisive authoritarian tactics.

Stemming the Rise of Global Populism

Democracy, despite not always offering immediate or flawless solutions, remains the most effective system for tackling the issues that concern the middle and working classes. While it has its imperfections, democracy empowers citizens to engage in the political landscape and to hold their representatives accountable. In a democratic setup, the populace holds the power to champion policies that address critical challenges such as income inequality and stagnant wages. This includes advocating for robust worker rights, enhancing educational opportunities and skill development, and implementing equitable tax systems.

Conversely, populism might present itself as a quick fix, but it often resorts to polarizing language and oversimplified answers that can intensify current issues and even lead to new complications.

Democracy, albeit sometimes slow and intricate, offers a structured platform for collective problem-solving, enabling citizens to unite and develop solutions that serve the wider community, not just a privileged minority. Therefore, while democracy is not devoid of shortcomings, it stands as the most effective system for ensuring that the voices of all citizens are considered and for collaboratively forging a more equitable and just society.

The recent surge in global populism has cast a spotlight on the growing discontent and marginalization within the middle class, a demographic often caught in the crosshairs of economic policies designed to favour the elite. This group, grappling with the realities of stagnant wages, precarious job security, and diminishing prospects for social mobility, has paradoxically become a fertile ground for the rise of populist and authoritarian leaders. These leaders, who profess to represent the 'common people,' often end up intensifying the very economic and social challenges their supporters face, deepening the sense of disillusionment and frustration, and continuing this vicious cycle by blaming externalities for the societal and economic problems they create.

Populist leaders, skilled in identifying and exploiting the widespread frustration, using tools as discussed earlier, within the middle class, position themselves as adversaries of what they portray as a detached and corrupt elite. They promise sweeping reforms and present themselves as the solution to rectify economic imbalances. However, their narrative is riddled with contradictions and oversimplifications. In practice, their policies often disproportionately benefit the wealthy, further exacerbating the economic inequalities they claim to oppose. Tax reforms and deregulation, staples of populist agendas, typically skew in favour of the affluent, undermining crucial social welfare programs and public services that are essential for the larger population, particularly the middle class.

The rise of populism, fueled by complex social and economic factors, signifies more than just a political upheaval; it's indicative of a deep-rooted socioeconomic crisis. This movement adeptly redirects public frustration, with populist figures skillfully steering this discontent towards tangential issues like immigration and societal shifts. Such redirection effectively shifts focus away from the fundamental economic challenges contributing to the erosion of the middle class. These leaders, by controlling the narrative, deflect responsibility away from economic policies that favor wealth accumulation among the elite, leading the public to erroneously ascribe their hardships to other, often unrelated, causes. However, history has shown that this approach is not indefinitely tenable. Eventually, reality catches up, revealing the underlying issues that have been overlooked or misrepresented.

Time and again, it has been shown that while populist leaders may adeptly channel public discontent towards peripheral issues, such as immigration or societal shifts, this often serves as a diversion from deep-seated economic and social problems. Such tactics, although they may provide temporary respite or a sense of vindication, have historically proven to be unsustainable. The Arab Spring, for instance, was a stark awakening to the repercussions of long-neglected economic hardships and social inequalities. Similarly, the Global Financial Crisis of 2008 laid bare the consequences of ignoring systemic financial risks. The fall of the Soviet Union and the Latin American Debt Crisis in the 1980s are further testaments to the eventual unraveling of systems that rely on misrepresentation and deflection of core socioeconomic issues. These historical precedents serve as a cautionary tale, highlighting the inevitable reckoning that follows when fundamental problems are overlooked or misrepresented in favor of populist rhetoric and their short-term promises.

The appeal of populism lies in its presentation of seemingly straightforward solutions to complex societal problems, particularly appealing during times of economic hardship. Yet, as shown, the outcomes of populist policies often fall short of their promises, leading the middle class into deeper economic adversity. As wealth continues to accumulate at the top echelons of society, the erosion of social safety nets, designed to protect the most vulnerable, exacerbates the challenges facing the middle class. This erosion not only impacts immediate financial stability but also has long-term implications for social mobility and the overall health of the middle class.

Moreover, the rise of global populism has introduced significant challenges to the foundations of democratic institutions and norms. Populist leaders, often under the pretext of embodying the "will of the people," display authoritarian tendencies that weaken the essential checks and balances of democratic governance. Their concentration of power in the executive branch, coupled with efforts to discredit the media and other democratic institutions, erodes public trust in these critical pillars of democracy. This erosion of trust and authority in democratic institutions marks a troubling shift towards a more centralised and potentially autocratic form of governance.

The diminution of civil liberties and rights is another alarming consequence of the rise of populism. Populist regimes often exploit the principle of majority rule to marginalize or suppress minority voices and interests, undermining the pluralistic and inclusive nature that is central to many democratic societies. This exploitation leads to the weakening of institutions that are vital for upholding democracy, as populist leaders install loyalists in key positions, compromising impartiality and competence in favour of allegiance and ideological conformity. This trend towards authoritarianism not only degrades the quality of democratic governance but also risks a regression into more autocratic forms of rule, where accountability, rule of law, and minority rights are severely compromised.

A key tactic employed by would-be authoritarian leaders is projection, a psychological and rhetorical strategy used to consolidate power and manipulate public perception. This involves attributing one's own undesirable traits or behaviours to others, particularly opponents or marginalised groups. By engaging in such projection, leaders deflect criticism from themselves and justify authoritarian actions, shaping public opinion, exacerbating social divisions, and undermining the foundational trust in democratic institutions.

Populist rhetoric's inherent contradictions expose a complex and troubling reality. While these leaders resonate with the middle class through their promises of change and economic revival, their policies and actions often lead to further economic disparities, social fragmentation, and an erosion of democratic principles. Addressing these issues requires societies to cultivate an informed and engaged citizenry capable of critically evaluating political narratives and their broader implications. Navigating the socioeconomic challenges brought forth by populism demands a collective effort towards more inclusive, equitable, and sustainable solutions that truly serve the interests of the broader population.

The rise of populism and its impact on the middle class and democratic institutions can be observed through various practical examples across different geographies. Here are some notable instances:

United States

Populist Leader: Donald Trump

Impact on Middle Class: Trump's tax reforms, particularly the Tax Cuts and Jobs Act of 2017, largely benefited corporations and the wealthy, with limited long-term benefits for the middle class. This widened the wealth gap.

Impact on Democratic Institutions: Trump's presidency saw challenges to democratic norms, including attacks on the media, claims of election fraud without evidence, and the undermining of trust in the electoral process, culminating in the Capitol insurrection on January 6, 2021. This democratic erosion continues in the "Stolen Election" rhetoric that continues to destabilise the US.

United Kingdom

Populist Movement: Brexit

Impact on Middle Class: Brexit, driven by populist rhetoric around reclaiming sovereignty and controlling immigration, has led to economic uncertainties, with potential long-term impacts on trade, employment, and prices that affect the middle class.

Impact on Democratic Institutions: Brexit revealed deep divisions in the UK, with significant debates on parliamentary sovereignty versus the public vote, and Scotland's increased calls for independence.

The emerging negative consequences of Brexit include economic challenges such as trade disruptions, increased bureaucracy, and a decline in foreign investment. There have been impacts on labour shortages, particularly in sectors reliant on EU workers. Political tensions have risen, notably in Northern Ireland, affecting the region's stability. Additionally, Brexit has led to increased costs for businesses and consumers, and complexities in UK-EU relations.

Brazil

Populist Leader: Jair Bolsonaro

Impact on Middle Class: Bolsonaro's economic policies, including pension reforms and budget cuts, have been controversial. While claiming to be aimed at boosting the economy, they have also raised concerns about social inequality and the future of public services.

Impact on Democratic Institutions: Bolsonaro has shown a tendency to undermine democratic norms, including attacking the press and showing disregard for environmental regulations and human rights, especially concerning indigenous communities.

Hungary

Populist Leader: Viktor Orbán

Impact on Middle Class: Orbán's economic policies have been mixed, with some growth but also accusations of cronyism and corruption, potentially limiting broader economic opportunities for the middle class.

Impact on Democratic Institutions: Orbán's government has been criticized for eroding democratic institutions, consolidating power, restricting press freedom, and weakening the judiciary's independence.

Turkey

Populist Leader: Recep Tayyip Erdoğan

Impact on Middle Class: Erdoğan's economic policies initially led to growth, but recent years have seen currency depreciation and inflation, affecting the middle class's purchasing power.

Impact on Democratic Institutions: Erdoğan's tenure has seen significant consolidation of power, especially after the 2016 coup attempt, with crackdowns on the media, opposition, and academia, leading to concerns about democratic backsliding.

Poland

Populist Party: Law and Justice Party (PiS)

Impact on Middle Class: PiS's social spending programs have been popular, but there are concerns about long-term economic sustainability and the impact on the country's fiscal position.

Impact on Democratic Institutions: PiS has been criticized for judicial reforms that undermine the independence of the judiciary, posing a threat to the rule of law and separation of powers.

These examples reflect a pattern where populist movements and leaders, while appealing to the middle class with promises of economic revival and national pride, often lead to policies that do not adequately address the middle class's long-term interests and instead pose significant challenges to democratic institutions and norms.

Historically, the rise of populist authoritarians and fascists has been a recurring theme in various contexts, each uniquely shaped by their sociopolitical and economic environments. Each with disastrous outcomes. Here are some notable historical examples:

Italy

Leader: Benito Mussolini

Impact on Society: Mussolini's regime promoted extreme nationalism and suppression of opposition, leading to social repression and a loss of civil liberties. His alignment with Nazi Germany contributed to Italy's involvement in World War II, resulting in widespread destruction and loss of life.

Impact on Democratic Institutions: Mussolini established a totalitarian state, dismantling democratic institutions and replacing them with fascist autocracy.

Germany

Leader: Adolf Hitler

Impact on Society: Hitler's regime was responsible for the Holocaust, leading to the genocide of millions. His aggressive expansionism triggered World War II, causing immense global destruction and loss of life.

Impact on Democratic Institutions: Hitler eradicated democracy, established a totalitarian regime, and suppressed all forms of opposition.

Spain

Leader: Francisco Franco

Impact on Society: Franco's dictatorship was marked by the violent repression of opposition, leading to social unrest and human rights abuses.

Impact on Democratic Institutions: Franco established an authoritarian regime that stifled political freedom and censored media.

Soviet Union

Leader: Joseph Stalin

Impact on Society: Stalin's rule was characterized by purges, forced labour camps, famines, and millions of deaths, leading to widespread social and economic disruption.

Impact on Democratic Institutions: Stalin established a totalitarian regime, suppressed political dissent, and controlled all aspects of life through the Communist Party.

China

Leader: Mao Zedong

Impact on Society: Mao's policies, including the Great Leap Forward and the Cultural Revolution, resulted in economic catastrophe, social chaos, and millions of deaths.

Impact on Democratic Institutions: Mao's leadership saw the entrenchment of Communist Party control over the state and society, undermining democratic principles.

Argentina

Leader: Juan Perón

Impact on Society: Perón's economic policies led to instability and debt, affecting the middle class. His initial social reforms later gave way to economic challenges.

Impact on Democratic Institutions: Perón's rule saw a decline in democratic institutions, characterized by political repression and media censorship.

Cuba

Leader: Fidel Castro

Impact on Society: Castro's regime was marked by the suppression of dissent, economic hardships, and a significant exodus of Cubans seeking better opportunities abroad.

Impact on Democratic Institutions: Castro established a one party state with widespread control over all aspects of life and a lack of political freedoms.

Iraq

Leader: Saddam Hussein

Impact on Society: Hussein's regime was notorious for human rights abuses and aggressive regional policies that led to wars and internal repression. Saddam Hussein's regime in Iraq was responsible for significant atrocities against its own citizens. The most infamous of these was the Halabja chemical attack in 1988, where Iraqi forces used chemical weapons on the Kurdish town of Halabja, resulting in the deaths of thousands, estimated between 3,200 and 5,000. Additionally, Saddam's regime carried out the Anfal Campaign against the Kurds, causing tens of thousands of deaths and destroying many villages.

Impact on Democratic Institutions: Saddam's governance was characterized by authoritarian rule with little regard for democratic processes or human rights.

Venezuela

Leader: Hugo Chávez

Impact on Society: Chávez's socialist policies initially improved social spending but later led to economic mismanagement, hyperinflation, and a humanitarian crisis.

Impact on Democratic Institutions: Chávez's rule saw an erosion of democratic institutions, media censorship, and politicization of the judiciary.

Each of these cases illustrates the complex interplay between populist or authoritarian leadership, societal impact, and the detrimental effects on democratic structures and institutions.

In conclusion, countering the rise of global populism necessitates a thorough and critical evaluation of populist rhetoric and a steadfast commitment to equitable and sustainable solutions that genuinely address the needs and aspirations of the middle class. This endeavour involves reinforcing democratic institutions, upholding the rule of law, and safeguarding minority rights. Through a concerted effort to preserve and promote democratic values and practices, the true aspirations of the middle class can be realized, ensuring the preservation of the integrity and vitality of democratic societies worldwide.

Empowering Voices

In envisioning a democratic way of governing that pivots away from the traditional top-down model dominated by a select group of elites, the focus shifts towards a system where power is more evenly distributed among ordinary citizens. This model emphasizes community organization as a foundational element, encouraging citizens to form local groups and associations that directly advocate for their interests and concerns. These grassroots organizations would become instrumental in shaping the political agenda, reflecting the collective will of the community.

A key feature of this approach is the implementation of direct democracy mechanisms. Citizens would have the opportunity to vote directly on policy issues through referendums and citizen initiatives. This system reduces the reliance on elected representatives as the sole decision-makers, placing more power in the hands of the people to shape policies that affect their lives.

Technology plays a crucial role in facilitating this democratic model. Digital platforms can be used to enhance participation, making the political process more accessible and inclusive. These platforms could host debates, conduct polls, and facilitate decision-making, allowing a wider segment of the population to engage in governance.

In addressing leadership challenges within a bottom-up democracy, incorporating the concept of rotating coaches, akin to mentors or guides, can play a significant role. These coaches would provide guidance and support to leaders and non-leaders, ensuring they stay aligned with the community's goals and values. Coaches are "commoners" that are chosen by those being coached based on a variety of criteria as selected by the coached.

Transparency in decision-making is crucial. Open and transparent processes allow community members to stay informed about decisions and actions taken by leaders. Coaches can assist leaders in maintaining this transparency, offering advice on effective communication and ethical decision-making. In this system, coaches are not all knowing advisors, but mirrors and feedback providers, when requested.

Rotating leadership positions is another key strategy. Regularly changing who holds leadership roles prevents the consolidation of power and keeps the leadership dynamic. Coaches can support new leaders as they transition into their roles, offering insights and advice based on their experiences.

Establishing term limits for leadership positions ensures that power is not held by any one individual or group for too long. Coaches can help leaders maximize their impact during their tenure and prepare them for the transition when their term ends. Also, leaders are not members of parties but individuals that put their hands-up for a stint in leadership and are voted for by a committee, also independently and individually chosen by the people with different tenure cadences.

Implementing checks and balances within the system is essential, coaches can serve as impartial observers, helping to identify any imbalances and suggesting corrective actions.

Community oversight is pivotal. Members actively participate in monitoring leaders and holding them accountable. Coaches can facilitate this process by helping to set up review mechanisms and encouraging open dialogue between leaders and community members.

In this democratic model, coaches are not just advisors to the leaders; they are integral to the system of governance itself. They help maintain a balance of power, ensure adherence to the community's principles, and support both leaders and community members. This approach democratizes leadership and fosters a sense of shared responsibility, making the community stronger and more cohesive.

The principles of decentralized organization, inspired by models operating without traditional hierarchies, emphasize equality, self-governance, and mutual support. Leadership in this context is based on service and responsibility rather than power, with collective decision-making and consensus-building at its core.

In this democratic model, a key feature is the incorporation of mechanisms for ongoing adaptation and improvement. This approach ensures that the system of governance remains dynamic and attuned to the changing needs of the community.

Central to this process are regular community assemblies, which serve as platforms for open discussion and decision-making. These gatherings are an opportunity for members to come together, review current guidelines and protocols, and collectively deliberate on necessary modifications. These assemblies would be a space for transparent communication and shared decision-making.

During these assemblies, members can voice their views, offer suggestions, and participate in discussions about the direction and functioning of the community. This participatory process is crucial in ensuring that all voices are heard and that decisions are made democratically. The Leaders of these assemblies are selected by the group of one assembly, for the next assembly. This is done by the group confirming the first person that puts their hand up.

Always focusing on the issue and not the person, the process of continual review and modification also involves assessing the effectiveness of existing governance structures. This model encourages the community to regularly evaluate how well the governance system is meeting its objectives. Are the needs of all members being addressed? Are there areas where improvements can be made? These are some of the questions that would be explored during the assemblies.

This dynamic approach to governance ensures that the system does not become stagnant or disconnected from the community's current realities. It allows for flexibility and responsiveness, enabling the community to adapt to new challenges and opportunities as they arise. The emphasis on collective decision-making and regular reassessment fosters a sense of ownership and engagement among community members, ensuring that the governance system remains truly representative and effective in serving the community's needs.

Servant leadership, as a distinct leadership style, adds a vital dimension to the envisioned democratic model. This approach shifts the focus from traditional hierarchical leadership to one that centres on serving the needs of others and empowering them to make decisions. By integrating servant leadership into the fabric of this bottom-up democracy, the model promotes more collaborative and community-driven decision-making, addressing some of the inherent shortcomings of traditional representative systems.

Servant leaders are characterized by their commitment to listening and understanding the needs and perspectives of community members. They prioritize the empowerment of individuals, enabling them to take ownership of their work and contribute meaningfully to decision-making processes. This style of leadership fosters a stronger sense of trust and collaboration within the community, as leaders are seen not as authoritative figures but as facilitators and supporters of the collective will.

By implementing servant leadership principles, the decision-making process becomes more effective and sustainable. It encourages a more holistic approach, where solutions are developed through a deeper understanding of the diverse needs and aspirations of the community members. This approach can lead to outcomes that are more widely accepted and supported, as they are the result of a genuinely participatory process.

While servant leadership alone may not resolve all the challenges of representative democracy, it offers a more inclusive and community-driven approach. This style of leadership can significantly contribute to addressing some of the democratic system's shortcomings by fostering a culture of mutual respect, empowerment, and active participation.

Ultimately, the success of a democratic system hinges on promoting a culture of transparency, accountability, and inclusion. It is crucial to ensure that all voices within the community are heard and respected and that decision-making is a shared responsibility. Integrating servant leadership into this democratic framework can play a significant role in achieving these objectives, paving the way for a more equitable, responsive, and engaged form of governance.

There are several prominent examples of individuals who have been recognized as servant leaders, both in historical and contemporary contexts. These leaders are known for their focus on serving others, empowering their teams or communities, and leading by example.

Jacinda Ardern - The Prime Minister of New Zealand is often cited as a contemporary example of servant leadership. Her response to the COVID-19 pandemic and the Christchurch mosque shootings demonstrated her empathetic approach, focus on the well-being of her people, and commitment to decisive, compassionate leadership.

Mahatma Gandhi - Gandhi is often cited as a quintessential servant leader. His leadership in India's struggle for independence was marked by non-violence, humility, and a focus on serving the greater good. He empowered millions to join in a collective movement for change, always placing the needs and well-being of others above his own.

Nelson Mandela - As the first Black President of South Africa and a key figure in the fight against apartheid, Mandela demonstrated servant leadership through his dedication to reconciliation, equality, and empowering the disenfranchised. Even after 27 years in prison, his focus remained on serving his country and its people to build a more inclusive society.

Mother Teresa - Known for her humanitarian work, Mother Teresa dedicated her life to serving the poor, sick, and dying. Her leadership style was characterized by compassion, selflessness, and a deep commitment to uplifting the most vulnerable sections of society.

Martin Luther King Jr. - A prominent leader in the American Civil Rights Movement, King exemplified servant leadership through his dedication to nonviolent activism and his focus on serving the cause of civil rights and social justice. He inspired and mobilized thousands with his vision and commitment to serving others.

Abraham Lincoln - As the 16th President of the United States, Lincoln demonstrated servant leadership through his commitment to preserving the Union and abolishing slavery. His empathy, humility, and willingness to listen to different perspectives were key elements of his leadership style.

Greg Mortenson - Greg is a humanitarian and social entrepreneur renowned for his commitment to peace and education in remote regions of Pakistan and Afghanistan. Through the Central Asia Institute, he has established hundreds of schools and educational programs, significantly impacting the lives of tens of thousands of children, especially girls. Mortenson champions education as a crucial instrument for peace and understanding, and his efforts have earned him prestigious accolades, including Pakistan's highest civilian award, the Sitara-e-Pakistan, and the Jefferson Award for Public Service. His vision has catalyzed a global movement advocating education as a pathway to peace, leaving an enduring influence that motivates others to contribute positively to their communities.

These leaders exemplify the principles of servant leadership through their dedication to the well-being of others, their focus on empowering and uplifting their communities, and their commitment to leading by example. They demonstrate that effective leadership is not about wielding power, but about serving and enabling others.

The focus in this model of governance is on serving the community and upholding collective responsibility, fostering a culture where each member contributes to the greater good. This approach offers a vision of governance that is inclusive, responsive, and reflective of the collective will of the people, marking a shift towards a more equitable distribution of power and a system where every citizen has a meaningful stake in decision-making processes.

Let's look at some examples of communities, groups, and political movements that have adopted participatory and collective approaches, along with their tangible successes:

Participatory Budgeting Movements - Cities like Porto Alegre in Brazil and New York City in the United States have implemented participatory budgeting, where residents directly decide on the allocation of municipal funds. In Porto Alegre, this approach significantly improved public amenities, with a marked increase in sewer and water connections and schools built through this process. In New York City, thousands of residents have voted on projects such as park improvements, school technology upgrades, and public housing repairs.

Cooperative Business Models - The Mondragon Corporation in Spain is a federation of worker cooperatives and one of the largest business groups in Spain. It's a significant success story, providing employment to over 74,000 people and demonstrating that cooperative, participatory business models can scale effectively while maintaining worker ownership and decision-making.

Doctors Without Borders (Médecins Sans Frontières) - Médecins Sans Frontières operate with a decentralized structure, allowing for quick response and effective action in crisis situations. Their success in providing medical aid in conflict zones and disaster areas, often with rapid deployment and high efficiency, is a testament to the effectiveness of their organizational structure.

Grassroots Political Movements - The Green Party, particularly in Europe, has seen electoral successes while advocating for environmental issues and social justice through grassroots participation. For instance, the German Green Party has been a part of coalitions in the national government and has influenced significant environmental policy decisions.

Community-Led Development Projects - The Grameen Bank in Bangladesh, a microfinance organization and community development bank, has successfully empowered countless rural women through microloans. By giving community members control over their financial decisions, Grameen Bank has significantly improved the economic conditions of many families and communities in Bangladesh.

Intentional Communities and Ecovillages - The Findhorn Ecovillage in Scotland is an example of a successful intentional community. It has achieved sustainability in living, with its ecological houses, organic food production, and renewable energy systems. The community is a model for sustainable living practices and has a global educational outreach.

The Royal Flying Doctor Service (RFDS) - RFDS in Australia exemplifies the effectiveness and essential nature of non-profit organizations in addressing critical community needs. Established in 1928 to provide emergency and primary health care services to remote and rural areas of Australia, the RFDS operates a fleet of aircraft equipped with medical facilities, effectively transforming the vast outback into a 'flying hospital.' This service overcomes the challenges posed by Australia's enormous distances, delivering lifesaving medical assistance and routine health care to communities otherwise isolated from such services. The RFDS's impact is profound, offering not only emergency medical evacuations but also essential primary health care, dental care, and mental health services to those living in remote regions. The success of the RFDS demonstrates how non-profit organizations can provide vital services, particularly in areas where government or private sector involvement is limited, underscoring their indispensable role in fostering equitable health care access and improving lives in communities across Australia.

Switzerland and Referenda - Switzerland stands as a prime example of direct democracy in action. The country's system of frequent referenda allows citizens to vote directly on a wide range of legislative and constitutional issues. This approach empowers Swiss people to have a significant say in their nation's laws and policies, leading to a highly engaged and politically active citizenry. It's a model that showcases how a society can successfully integrate direct democracy into a modern governmental framework, ensuring that the voice of the populace plays a central role in shaping national decisions. The success of this system is reflected in the high level of public participation and the responsive nature of Swiss governance to the needs and opinions of its citizens.

Maverick Company - Maverick, known for its unconventional business model, exemplifies how a company can thrive by deviating from traditional corporate practices. Emphasizing a flat organizational structure, Maverick encourages employee autonomy, empowerment, and participation in decision-making processes. This approach has led to increased innovation, employee satisfaction, and productivity. The company's success demonstrates the effectiveness of non-hierarchical management and the value of prioritizing employee input and engagement in corporate culture. Maverick serves as a model for businesses worldwide, showing that fostering a collaborative and inclusive work environment can drive both employee well-being and business success.

Bhutan - Bhutan's Gross National Happiness Index (GHI) represents a novel approach to national development, prioritizing the well-being and happiness of its citizens over traditional economic metrics like GDP. This holistic model is structured around four pillars: sustainable socio-economic development, cultural preservation, environmental conservation, and good governance. Tangible achievements include significant environmental protections, with a majority of the country forested, advancements in renewable energy, and the maintenance of cultural heritage. Bhutan has also made strides in healthcare and education, providing free access to all citizens, leading to improvements in life expectancy and literacy rates. The overall unemployment rate in Bhutan has been around 2-3% in recent years. In contrast, the unemployment rate in the United States fluctuates more significantly, influenced by economic cycles, but it generally hovers around 4-6% in recent years.

These examples illustrate how participatory and collective decision-making models can lead to tangible successes, from improved public amenities and successful large-scale cooperatives to effective crisis response by NGOs and impactful environmental and community policies by political movements. They demonstrate that alternative governance structures, focusing on direct participation and community involvement, can achieve significant and meaningful results.

This perspective highlights a fundamental debate in societal and organizational structures; the value of quality of life, respect, support, and humanity versus the exclusive pursuit of wealth and power, often associated with traditional hierarchical systems. This dichotomy presents two distinct visions of success and leadership.

In traditional hierarchical structures, success is traditionally measured in terms of wealth accumulation, power, and influence. Leaders in such systems are often celebrated for their financial achievements, corporate growth, and competitive dominance. These structures can be efficient in terms of economic output and organizational control, but they overlook the well-being and dignity of individuals, especially those at the lower rungs of the hierarchy.

On the other hand, models that prioritize quality of life, mutual respect, and humanity offer a different definition of success. Here, the emphasis is on creating supportive, inclusive communities and workplaces where everyone's contributions are valued. Success is measured not just in economic terms but also in the well-being of individuals and the strength of the community. Leaders in such models are recognized for their empathy, ability to empower others, and commitment to social and environmental responsibility.

This perspective aligns with the growing movement towards more equitable and sustainable ways of living and working. It reflects a shift in priorities, where the focus is on creating systems that nurture human potential, foster respect and support among individuals, and operate with a sense of responsibility towards society and the environment.

This viewpoint opines that while traditional hierarchical structures may continue to have their proponents, there is a significant and growing interest in alternative models that offer a more humane and supportive approach to governance and leadership. This shift is not about rejecting financial wealth, but about reimagining what it means to lead, succeed, and thrive in a society that values every individual's dignity and well-being as well as protecting or even encouraging high quality of living including the financial kind.

Ancient tribes typically exhibited a more bottom-up organization, characterized by several key features in their governance and social structure. Decisions within these communities were often made collectively, either through a consensus approach in community gatherings or by councils of elders, allowing for broad participation in decision-making. Leadership roles in tribes were often based on passion, wisdom, experience, or specific skills, and were not rigidly fixed. Leaders in these societies functioned more as facilitators or coordinators for the community's needs rather than as authoritative figures, and sometimes, these roles were temporary or task-specific.

The social fabric of tribal societies was built on mutual aid and cooperation. Resources and responsibilities were usually shared among members, with a focus on the collective well-being of the tribe. Rather than a formalized legal system, many tribes governed themselves through customs, traditions, and unwritten rules, collectively upheld and modified as needed. This reflects a system where social norms and rules emerge organically from the community.

While some tribes had hierarchical elements, especially in larger or more complex societies, these structures were generally less pronounced compared to centralized states. Hierarchies that did exist were often more about social roles and responsibilities than rigid power structures. In summary, the organization of ancient tribes leaned towards a community-centric model, emphasizing collective decision-making, shared responsibilities, and leadership that served the needs of the group.

In challenging the notion that hierarchy and inequality are essential drivers of technological and societal advancement, we look to the insights of David Wengrow and David Graeber. Their research provides a compelling argument that past civilizations, often non-hierarchical in nature, achieved significant milestones, contradicting the commonly held belief that progress is a product of capitalist structures and societal hierarchies.

Wengrow and Graeber's exploration of human history, as presented in "The Dawn of Everything," reveals a diverse tapestry of social organizations that were innovative and complex, yet not necessarily reliant on rigid hierarchical systems. They illustrate that human societies have not always followed a linear progression from primitive equality to complex inequality. Instead, they argue that many early societies displayed remarkable levels of sophistication and innovation, even in the absence of the strict hierarchies and inequalities that characterize modern capitalist systems.

One of the key examples provided by Wengrow and Graeber is the Indigenous North American populations, whose encounters with European settlers offered a critique of European hierarchy and patriarchy. These indigenous societies presented alternative models of organization, which were more egalitarian yet no less sophisticated. This perspective directly influenced European thought in the 18th century, challenging the then-prevailing notions about the superiority of hierarchical structures.

The authors also delve into the archaeological and anthropological evidence from various parts of the world, which demonstrates that early urban settlements and civilizations often existed with minimal signs of social hierarchy. These societies were able to build cities, develop agriculture, and create complex social structures without the centralized power and inequality that many assume to be necessary for such achievements.

Their research documents early cities that showed little or no evidence of social hierarchies, lacking traditional markers like temples, palaces, central storage facilities, or written administration. This finding suggests urban settlements could develop and thrive without rigid structures of hierarchy and centralization.

A notable example is Teotihuacan, an ancient city that initially exhibited hierarchical structures but later adopted a more egalitarian trajectory, providing high-quality housing for most of its citizens. This evolution within Teotihuacan demonstrates societies' potential to transform towards social equality.

Tlaxcala, before European arrival, serves as an example of Indigenous urban democracy in the Americas. This society had democratic institutions such as municipal councils and popular assemblies, showcasing a decentralized and participatory form of urban organization.

In ancient Mesopotamia, democratic institutions were present, challenging the view that early urban civilizations were predominantly hierarchical and autocratic.

Wengrow and Graeber also delve into the diversity and complexity of political life among non-agricultural societies across continents, including Japan and the Americas. These societies displayed a range of social structures, from monumental architecture to the conscious rejection of slavery through cultural schismogenesis, indicating a rich variety of social experiments.

Contrary to the concept of a sudden 'Agricultural Revolution,' the authors argue for a narrative of slow change and ecological flexibility in agriculture's adoption. This gradual process allowed for sustained biodiversity and did not always lead to demographic collapse or the emergence of hierarchical structures.

These examples collectively suggest that early human societies were capable of significant innovation and complexity in their social structures without necessarily depending on centralized authority or marked social inequality. Wengrow and Graeber's work challenges traditional views of societal advancement and opens up new perspectives on the potential forms of human organization.

In summary, Wengrow and Graeber's work provides a nuanced understanding of human history, showing that non-hierarchical and more egalitarian forms of social organization have been both prevalent and successful. Their research challenges the conventional wisdom that inequality and hierarchical structures are prerequisites for societal advancement and technological innovation. This perspective invites us to reconsider the paths of human progress and the potential of alternative forms of social organization in achieving complex and sophisticated societies.

AI & Virality for Social Change

Harnessing the Digital Wave: The '99%' Revolutionizing the Information Battlefield

In an age dominated by digital media, the power of information has never been more potent. For the '99%', this presents both a challenge and an opportunity in their quest for social justice and equality. The principles of virality, once the domain of well-resourced elites, are now tools that can be wielded by the masses to counteract prevailing narratives and disseminate alternative viewpoints.

AI technologies have revolutionized the way information is processed, analyzed, and disseminated. By leveraging AI, the '99%' can sift through vast amounts of data to identify trends, understand public sentiments, and tailor messages that resonate with diverse audiences. AI can help predict which messages are likely to be effective and identify the best platforms and times for dissemination. This targeted approach ensures that the message not only reaches a wide audience but also strikes a chord with them.

Alongside AI, the concept of virality is crucial in the digital age. Viral content has the power to reach millions of people rapidly, transcending geographical and social barriers. By creating content that is emotionally resonant, easily shareable, and aligned with the values and experiences of the '99%', movements can ignite conversations and foster a sense of solidarity among diverse groups.

In the complex realm of digital communication, the '99%' face significant challenges, particularly in dealing with the widespread issues of sensationalism and misinformation, often utilized by the elite to distract and mislead. Addressing these challenges requires a comprehensive and strategic approach.

Sensationalism thrives on exaggerated or emotionally charged content, designed to grab attention and manipulate public opinion. To counter this, the '99%' can launch media literacy campaigns aimed at educating the public on how to identify and critically evaluate sensationalist tactics. These campaigns can take various forms, such as workshops, online resources, and interactive courses, equipping individuals with the skills to discern bias and recognize manipulative strategies in media.

Misinformation, which involves the deliberate spreading of false information, poses a more insidious threat. It can distort public discourse and shape perceptions based on falsehoods. Tackling this requires robust fact-checking initiatives. Collaborating with or establishing independent fact-checking bodies can play a crucial role in verifying claims, especially those widely circulated on social media. The findings from these fact-checks can then be disseminated through the networks of the '99%' to counter false narratives with verified, accurate information.

Navigating the biases inherent in digital platforms is another critical aspect. These platforms often control which content gains visibility and which does not, through their algorithms. This can lead to the marginalization of voices that challenge prevailing narratives. To overcome this, the '99%' can diversify their digital presence, using a mix of mainstream and alternative platforms to disseminate their message. This includes not only popular social media channels but also independent media sites, forums, and custom platforms dedicated to open discourse.

Engaging effectively with the algorithms of major platforms can also enhance the visibility of their message. Understanding and applying SEO techniques, timing posts strategically for optimal engagement, and using hashtags cleverly can increase the reach and impact of their content.

Creating content that is both high-quality and engaging is crucial for cutting through the digital noise. Employing compelling visuals, storytelling, and relatable narratives can make the message more appealing and memorable. Additionally, collaborating with influencers and community leaders who have significant online followings can further amplify the message. These individuals can lend their credibility and reach to the movement, helping to spread the message to a wider audience.

By adopting these multifaceted strategies, the '99%' can effectively combat the challenges posed by sensationalism and misinformation in the digital sphere. This approach ensures that their message is not only heard but also resonates with a broad audience, driving meaningful engagement and inspiring action towards social change.

Building digital communities that support and amplify the message of the '99%', can serve as hubs for sharing information, coordinating actions, and providing mutual support. The role of influencers and community leaders in shaping public opinion and mobilizing support is also explored, emphasizing the importance of credible and relatable voices in driving change.
Building digital communities plays a pivotal role in amplifying the message of the '99%', creating spaces where information, ideas, and support can circulate freely among like-minded individuals. These communities function as dynamic hubs that not only disseminate information but also coordinate collective actions and foster a sense of solidarity among members.

In the digital age, communities are often formed on various online platforms, including social media groups, forums, and dedicated websites. These spaces allow for the exchange of ideas and experiences, enabling members to stay informed about issues, discuss strategies, and mobilize for collective action. For instance, an online forum dedicated to workers' rights might share information about labour laws, organize virtual events for awareness, and coordinate real-world protests or advocacy campaigns.

An essential aspect of these communities is their ability to provide mutual support. In a world where individual struggles can often feel isolating, digital communities offer a sense of belonging and collective strength. They can be particularly empowering for individuals in remote or underserved areas, who might otherwise lack access to supportive networks.

The role of influencers and community leaders within these digital spaces is critical. These individuals often have substantial followings and can leverage their platforms to bring attention to the causes championed by the '99%'. By sharing content, engaging in discussions, and endorsing initiatives, influencers can significantly boost the visibility and credibility of the movement.

Community leaders, on the other hand, are instrumental in maintaining the cohesion and effectiveness of these digital communities. They moderate discussions, ensure the flow of accurate information and foster a constructive and supportive environment. They also play a key role in organizing and directing the collective energy of the community towards specific goals or actions.

However, for influencers and community leaders to be effective, they need to be credible and relatable. Credibility is established through consistent, accurate, and transparent communication. It involves backing up claims with evidence, acknowledging uncertainties, and being honest about intentions and affiliations. Relatability is equally important; leaders and influencers who share personal stories or demonstrate an understanding of the everyday experiences of their audience can form stronger connections and inspire greater engagement.

These digital communities, under the guidance of credible leaders and influencers, become more than just platforms for information sharing; they transform into powerful forces for change. They can organize impactful campaigns, influence public opinion, and even affect policy decisions. As such, building and nurturing these communities is a vital strategy for the '99%' in their endeavour to create a more equitable and just society.

Taylor Swift, a globally recognized artist, has significantly engaged in political and social issues, particularly in the United States, to support democracy and counteract populism. Initially known for keeping a relatively apolitical public persona, Swift made a notable shift in 2018 when she endorsed Democratic candidates in Tennessee for the midterm elections. This marked a significant change in her approach, demonstrating her willingness to use her influence to promote values she supports. This was against advice by her inner circle who were worried about the impact on her brand, her earnings and even her safety. She went ahead anyway, standing for purpose and truth.

She has been particularly vocal about the importance of voting, urging her fans to register and participate in elections. Her appeals have led to a reported increase in voter registrations, especially among young people, thereby contributing to the strengthening of democratic processes. Swift has also used her social media platforms and public appearances to address various social issues, including advocating for LGBTQ+ rights and racial equality. Her statements align her with progressive movements that stand against discrimination and populism.

Apart from her public statements, Swift has been involved in legal battles that underline personal rights and freedoms. Her lawsuit against a radio DJ for sexual assault and her stance on owning the rights to her music send powerful messages about personal autonomy and resisting exploitation.

Furthermore, Swift's philanthropic efforts extend to supporting a range of causes, including education, disaster relief, LGBTQ+ rights, and women's rights. Through these actions, she leverages her platform to promote democratic values, civic participation, and social justice, reflecting a broader trend among celebrities using their status to influence societal and political conversations.

There are several other notable celebrities and public figures who have used their platforms to advocate for democracy, fight against populism, and engage in political and social activism, similar to Taylor Swift. These include:

Beyoncé (USA): Known for her influential music and performances, Beyoncé has been vocal about various social issues, including racial equality, gender equality, and voting rights. She has used her platform to support Black Lives Matter and encourage voter participation.

LeBron James (USA): The NBA superstar has been active in promoting social justice and political engagement. He started the "More Than a Vote" campaign, which aims to combat systemic, racist voter suppression by educating, energizing, and protecting the community.

Angelina Jolie (USA): As a UNHCR Special Envoy, Jolie has long been involved in humanitarian efforts worldwide. She has advocated for refugees' rights and brought attention to global conflict and displacement issues.

Lady Gaga (USA): Lady Gaga has been a strong advocate for LGBTQ+ rights and mental health awareness. Through her Born This Way Foundation, she has worked to empower youth, promote kindness, and create a more accepting society.

John Legend (USA): Legend has been actively involved in campaigns for criminal justice reform and education. He founded the FREE AMERICA campaign to change the national conversation about America's criminal justice policies and to end mass incarceration.

Jane Fonda (USA): An actress and activist, Fonda has been involved in social activism for decades, focusing on issues like climate change, peace, and women's rights. She has been arrested multiple times during her Fire Drill Fridays protests to bring attention to climate issues.

Emma Watson (United Kingdom): Known for her role in the Harry Potter series, amongst others, Watson has been a vocal advocate for gender equality. As a UN Women Goodwill ambassador, she launched the HeForShe campaign, encouraging men to advocate for gender equality.

Alicia Keys (USA): The singer-songwriter has been involved in various causes, including HIV/AIDS awareness and racial justice. She co-founded the non-profit organization Keep a Child Alive and has been active in the Black Lives Matter movement.

Malala Yousafzai (Pakistan): The youngest Nobel Prize laureate, Malala is known for her advocacy for girls' education in Pakistan and globally. She survived an assassination attempt by the Taliban and has since become a global figure in the fight for educational rights.

Greta Thunberg (Sweden): A young climate activist who gained international recognition for initiating the global "Fridays for Future" school strike movement, advocating for urgent action to address climate change.

Emma González (USA): A survivor of the Stoneman Douglas High School shooting, González became an advocate for gun control in the United States and co-founded the gun-control advocacy group Never Again MSD.

Aamir Khan (India): A prominent Bollywood actor, Khan has been involved in raising awareness about various social issues in India through his TV show "Satyamev Jayate." He has addressed topics like healthcare, education, and gender equality.

Angelique Kidjo (Benin): A Grammy Award-winning singer, Kidjo is a UNICEF Goodwill Ambassador who advocates for children's and women's rights in Africa and globally.

Bono (Ireland): The lead vocalist of U2, Bono is well-known for his activism in the fight against HIV/AIDS and poverty, particularly in Africa. He co-founded organizations like DATA, EDUN, the ONE Campaign, and Product Red.

Ricky Martin (Puerto Rico): An international pop star, Martin is an advocate for children's rights and the fight against human trafficking. He established the Ricky Martin Foundation to advocate for the wellbeing of children around the world.

Roger Federer (Switzerland): The tennis champion's Roger Federer Foundation supports educational projects in Southern Africa and Switzerland, focusing on improving access to quality early learning and basic education.

Nomzamo Mbatha (South Africa): An actress and human rights activist, Mbatha is known for her work with the United Nations High Commissioner for Refugees (UNHCR) in advocating for displaced people across Africa.

Daniel Radcliffe (United Kingdom): The actor, famous for his role in the "Harry Potter" series, has spoken out on various social issues and has been involved in charitable works, using his platform to promote inclusivity and tolerance.

J.K. Rowling (United Kingdom): The author of the "Harry Potter" series has been vocal on social media and in her public life about political issues, including democracy and human rights. Despite some controversy over her comments, she has consistently advocated for freedom of speech and expression.

Elton John (United Kingdom): The renowned musician is a vocal advocate for LGBTQ+ rights and has used his platform to promote equality and fight against populist rhetoric that marginalizes minority groups.

José Andrés (Spain): A chef and restaurateur, Andrés has become known for his humanitarian efforts through his non-profit organization World Central Kitchen. He has been involved in disaster relief efforts worldwide and advocates for food security and policies that support vulnerable populations.

Eno Peçi (Albania): A prominent ballet dancer, Peçi has used his art to promote cultural understanding and bridge gaps between communities. He has been involved in projects that foster unity and speak against divisive populist rhetoric.

Mads Mikkelsen (Denmark): The acclaimed actor has occasionally spoken out on political issues, promoting democratic values and open-mindedness in his public statements.

Giannis Antetokounmpo (Greece): The NBA star, originally from Greece, has become an influential figure in sports and beyond. He has used his platform to promote equality and social justice, which aligns with democratic values and counters populist narratives.

These celebrities and many others have followed in the footsteps of using their fame and influence to promote social change, advocate for human rights, and encourage civic engagement, demonstrating the potential impact of public figures in shaping societal and political narratives.

While individuals within the 99% may have limited resources compared to the affluent 1%, their combined financial power is substantial, offering a significant funding source for campaigns counteracting elite-driven narratives. Crowdfunding platforms, for instance, can facilitate mass funding initiatives, becoming pivotal tools in generating the capital necessary for such undertakings. Similarly, grassroots fundraising efforts, primarily consisting of small donations from a broad base, can accumulate significant funds while engaging communities, fostering a sense of ownership and commitment to the cause.

However, challenges arise due to the stark financial disparity between the 99% and the 1%. While the 99% has potential collective power, it often struggles to match the affluent's funding capabilities. Therefore, strategic planning and efficient resource management are imperative to allocate the collected funds effectively. Overcoming these financial obstacles not only requires understanding and leveraging the potential funding power within the 99% but also necessitates building awareness regarding the significant impact of collective funding.

Raising awareness can drive participation, with educational campaigns playing a crucial role in informing the public about how their small, pooled contributions can lead to significant societal changes. Furthermore, developing and promoting user-friendly donation platforms can simplify the contribution process, making it accessible and encouraging to a wider audience. Importantly, maintaining transparency and accountability in fund usage is essential for building and sustaining trust among contributors. Regular updates on how funds are used and the progress of various campaigns can further bolster participation and support, thereby harnessing the 99%'s collective financial strength to promote narratives of equity and fairness in the face of economically polarized societies.

In the quest for social change, the '99%' face the dual challenge of countering the dominant narratives of the elite '1%' and navigating the pervasive influence of sensationalism. The key lies in strategically harnessing AI and the principles of virality to craft and disseminate counter-narratives that resonate deeply with diverse demographic groups. AI's potential to understand public sentiments through data analytics and sentiment analysis is invaluable for creating engaging, relatable, and shareable content. This approach enhances the potential for widespread dissemination of narratives that champion the cause of the '99%', making them not only engaging but also emotionally resonant, thus increasing their chances of going viral.

In addition to financial strategies, the '99%' must adopt a multifaceted approach to rise above the drama propagated by the '1%'. This includes embracing compelling storytelling, fostering media literacy, utilizing AI to analyze content trends, promoting positive virality, collaborating with ethical media outlets, spotlighting solutions and actions, engaging communities, setting a tone of honest and transparent communication, actively combating misinformation, and presenting a unified front in messaging and goals.

Regaining Agency

This Chapter outlines vital strategies for the 99% to regain agency amidst a tumultuous information landscape. Through fostering critical thinking and media literacy, individuals become empowered to discern truths, navigate misinformation, and counter deceptive narratives effectively. Engaging in constructive dialogue and robust advocacy are pivotal, creating spaces for consensus and influencing policies towards justice and equity.

Furthermore, building a responsive and informed civic culture is crucial. This endeavor requires not only the active participation of the public in democratic processes but also a deep commitment to education that nurtures civic duty, critical analysis, and media literacy. As the 99% cultivates these skills and values, they not only reclaim agency but also actively contribute to crafting a society that mirrors their aspirations and needs, standing resilient against the manipulation exerted by the elite 1%.

In the arena of populist influence, we underscore the imperative for the 99% to regain agency through the enhancement of critical thinking and media literacy. In an age where information is easily manipulated and disseminated, these skills are not just beneficial but essential for navigating through the noise and discerning fact from fiction.

Critical thinking is vital in dissecting the messages that flow through various information channels. The 99% need to cultivate an analytical mindset that questions and evaluates the information received, considering the source's credibility, the evidence provided, and the logic behind the arguments made. This discerning approach helps to shield individuals from accepting misleading narratives that might be propagated by those in power for self-serving purposes.

Media literacy is a complementary tool that empowers the public to interpret and assess the content disseminated through various media platforms effectively. It involves understanding how media messages are crafted and for what purpose, recognizing the techniques used to enhance the appeal of messages, and identifying potential biases or misrepresentations. With heightened media literacy, individuals are better equipped to sift through the overwhelming volume of information encountered daily, distinguishing valuable insights from deceptive propaganda.

We advocate for a proactive approach to developing these skills within the 99%. Educational institutions, community groups, and individuals themselves should prioritize fostering critical thinking and media literacy as fundamental competencies for civic participation in the modern world. These tools arm the public with the ability to challenge and counteract manipulative narratives, thereby reclaiming their agency and actively participating in shaping a society that reflects their true needs and aspirations.

The torrent of misinformation and divisive narratives dispersed in the populist landscape makes it indispensable for the public to cultivate spaces for open, informed, and respectful discussion.

Constructive dialogue is essential for bridging divides, understanding different perspectives, and building consensus on vital issues. It demands active listening, empathetic engagement, and the willingness to reassess and possibly alter one's viewpoints based on new insights and understanding. This form of dialogue fosters an environment where misinformation and manipulative rhetoric can be challenged and dissected collaboratively, providing the community with a resilient defence against divisive populist strategies.

Moreover, advocacy plays a pivotal role in regaining agency. The 99% can harness the power of collective voice and action to advocate for policies and leadership that truly serve their interests and well-being. Advocacy initiatives should be grounded in factual information, a clear understanding of the issues at stake, and a commitment to promoting equity, justice, and social welfare. Whether it's through engaging with elected representatives, participating in community organizations, or using digital platforms to amplify their voices, individuals within the 99% can actively contribute to shaping the political and social landscape.

Through fostering constructive dialogue and active advocacy, "Silent Echoes" suggests that the 99% can not only protect themselves from the insidious influence of misinformation but also reclaim their rightful place in the decision-making processes that impact their lives. Engaging in these practices empowers individuals and communities to navigate through the complexities of the contemporary information environment, fostering a society that is more informed, cohesive, and resilient in the face of populist manipulation.

In navigating through the narratives presented, it becomes apparent that building a responsive and informed civic culture is imperative for the 99%. This not only serves as a bulwark against misinformation but also fosters an environment where democratic values and inclusive discussions thrive.

A responsive civic culture actively engages with the socio-political landscape, participating in dialogues, deliberations, and decision-making processes that shape society. It requires individuals to be attentive to and reflective of the issues that permeate their community and broader society. This responsiveness enables the public to swiftly and effectively counteract attempts by the elite 1% to manipulate narratives or implement policies that primarily serve their interests at the expense of the majority.

Creating an informed civic culture is equally critical. This involves cultivating a deep understanding and awareness of both current events and the historical context in which they occur. An informed populace is less susceptible to manipulation and more equipped to engage in meaningful discussions about the future of their society. This awareness should also extend to recognizing and deciphering the tactics used by populist leaders and the elite to sow discord and misinformation.

We advocate for a proactive approach to fostering a civic culture that is both responsive and informed. This involves investment in education that not only imparts knowledge but also nurtures critical thinking, media literacy, and a sense of civic duty. Moreover, there needs to be encouragement and support for institutions and platforms that facilitate open dialogue, debate, and the sharing of reliable information. Through these mechanisms, the 99% can reclaim their agency, actively participate in their democracy, and work collectively towards a more equitable and just society. This fortified civic culture becomes an essential asset in the continuous endeavour to understand, challenge, and ultimately dismantle the manipulative narratives spun by the elite 1%.

Vote, Vote, Vote!

However, in the pursuit of regaining agency, one of the most impactful tools at the disposal of the 99% is the exercise of their democratic right to vote. Learning from the Australian system of compulsory voting provides valuable insights into enhancing voter turnout and achieving more genuine representative results. In Australia, where voting is mandatory for eligible citizens, the voter turnout is consistently high (over 90% as opposed to an average of 67% in the US and India). This not only reflects a sense of civic duty but also ensures a more accurate representation of the diverse voices within the population.

Forced voting, as implemented in Australia, addresses the issue of voter apathy that can dilute the democratic process. When citizens are compelled to cast their votes, it leads to a more comprehensive and inclusive participation, capturing a broader spectrum of perspectives. This approach counters the tendency of some individuals to abstain from voting, ensuring that the outcomes of elections more faithfully mirror the collective will of the people.

Moreover, the Australian experience demonstrates that compulsory voting contributes to a political landscape where policies are crafted with a deeper understanding of the diverse needs and aspirations of the entire society. By embracing a system that encourages universal participation, the 99% can challenge the existing power dynamics and contribute to the establishment of a government that genuinely represents their interests.

Incorporating lessons from the Australian model into the strategies outlined in this chapter, we emphasize the pivotal role of voting as a tool for the 99% to actively shape their democratic environment. By fostering a culture that recognizes the importance of each individual's vote, we pave the way for a more inclusive and responsive democracy, ultimately strengthening the collective agency of the 99%.

Reclaiming the Silent Echoes

"Silent Echoes" delves into the covert mechanisms employed by the 1% to exert influence, often at the expense of the 99%, and provides a roadmap for reclaiming agency. The book uncovers the crafting of populist narratives and the dissemination of conspiracy theories as tools for consolidating power, deepening societal divisions, and perpetuating inequality. Beyond diagnosis, it prescribes concrete steps for empowerment, urging individuals and communities to embrace lifelong learning, critical thinking, open dialogue, and active civic participation as essential components of a genuinely democratic and equitable society.

"Silent Echoes" offers a comprehensive exploration of the strategies utilized by the elite 1% to control societal narratives. From spreading conspiracy theories to weaving persuasive populist narratives, these tactics serve a singular purpose: to amass and secure power and wealth, often to the detriment of the 99%. The book meticulously reveals how these dynamics unfold in real time, with tangible consequences for individuals and communities. It paints a stark picture where the majority are not merely sidelined but actively disenfranchised, leading to stark inequalities and manipulation by the affluent minority.

These insights illuminate the covert operations of the powerful, providing the 99% with the knowledge needed to navigate and counter these influences. Understanding these mechanisms is the first step towards liberation from manipulation's invisible chains, enabling the reclamation of agency. "Silent Echoes" functions as both a lens to comprehend hidden power dynamics and a guide for fostering a more inclusive, equitable, and genuinely democratic society where power is distributed and not concentrated.

Individual empowerment stands as a cornerstone for change, necessitating a commitment to lifelong learning and education. Knowledge is a powerful tool, enabling a profound understanding of the world's intricacies and nuances. The pursuit of learning empowers individuals to hone their critical thinking skills, allowing them to discern truth from misinformation, and contribute positively to societal discourse and action.

At the community level, "Silent Echoes" advocates for the creation and nurturing of spaces that foster open dialogue, transparent communication, and inclusive collaboration. Transparency and inclusivity are pivotal, as they form the foundation of trust and collective action. Through these collaborative efforts, communities not only protect themselves from divisive narratives but also create an environment where equity and justice are lived realities.

The book underscores the importance of concerted advocacy efforts. Advocacy, as portrayed in "Silent Echoes," is a collective endeavour that requires individuals and communities to join forces in calling for policies and practices that genuinely represent the majority's aspirations. Through active and informed advocacy, the silent echoes can resonate in the halls of power, influencing policy, challenging misinformation, and ensuring that the narrative landscape is not monopolized but is a reflection of diverse voices.

As "Silent Echoes" concludes, it leaves you with a hopeful yet grounded outlook. The book isn't just about painting a vision but about calling for the assertion of agency by the 99%. This is the vital step in crafting a future that is both democratic and equitable. The potential within the silent majority is what fuels this optimism; a treasure trove of tools, insights, and knowledge equipping you to reclaim their silenced voices and actively contribute to a society that embodies the values and needs of the majority.

Realizing this vision is not a passive endeavour but a commitment that demands continuous effort and collaboration. Each individual's contribution is vital to weaving a resilient, inclusive, and just society. Challenges will arise, but courage, determination, and the dismantling of the status quo are key to dismantling inequality and amplifying voices that were once silenced.

"Silent Echoes" encourages you to approach the future with courage and purpose, engaging with the structures around them, advocating for change, and contributing to the chorus of voices calling for transformation. Each echo, once silent, has the potential to reverberate through society, creating ripples of change that are both vibrant and transformative.

In closing, "Silent Echoes" serves as both a mirror reflecting the complexities of society and a guiding light toward empowerment and action. It not only diagnoses the present but prescribes a path to a future where echoes are not merely heard but actively shape the landscape; embodying the power and promise held within each individual.

Free Speech

Under the dappled shade of their favorite coffee shop tree, Alex and Jordan found themselves diving into a conversation that was both timely and complex. With their coffees in hand, they embarked on a discussion about the ever-blurring lines between free speech and hate speech.

Alex started, "You know, I've been pondering the real essence of free speech lately. It's a pillar of democracy, right? Enshrined in the First Amendment and the Universal Declaration of Human

Rights. It's all about the freedom to express even the most controversial or unpopular ideas."

Jordan, always ready for a thought-provoking discussion, nodded. "Yeah, that freedom is vital for a healthy society. But where does hate speech fit into this landscape?"

"That's the tricky part," Alex replied, "Hate speech, unlike free speech, specifically targets and demeans groups based on race, religion, or other inherent characteristics. It's often legally restricted because its intent is to incite harm or discrimination, which free speech doesn't encompass."

Jordan reflected on this distinction. "So, while we can express our opinions freely, there's a line we can't cross, especially when it leads to violence or threatens public safety?"

"Exactly," Alex said. "The legal and moral boundaries of free speech are pretty clear, but enforcing them, especially in today's digital age, is a whole other challenge."

Jordan leaned forward, "Speaking of the digital age, doesn't it seem like social media platforms sometimes permit hate speech? It's like they prioritize engagement and ad revenue over the ethical implications."

"You're hitting a nerve there," Alex agreed. "These platforms have become breeding grounds for hate speech, amplifying it under the guise of free speech. It's a dangerous game where the lines are blurred, and the harm is real."

"And there's this argument about wokeism," Jordan added, swirling his coffee. "Some say that any effort to limit hate speech is just being overly politically correct or 'woke', and that it stifles free speech."

"But that's a false narrative," Alex countered. "Combating hate speech isn't about suppressing free speech; it's about safeguarding individuals and communities from speech that's intentionally harmful. It's about maintaining a balance where freedom of expression doesn't mean freedom to harm."

Jordan nodded, "The context is so important, isn't it? What's considered hate speech in one culture or country might be seen as free speech in another. And each platform, each community, navigates these waters differently."

As their conversation meandered through the various nuances of the issue, they realized the immense challenge societies and platforms face. It wasn't just about legal definitions; it was about ethical responsibilities, societal norms, and the evolving landscape of communication in the digital era.

Their discussion didn't provide clear-cut solutions, but it underscored the need for ongoing dialogue and critical thinking in this complex interplay of speech, rights, and responsibilities. Finishing their coffees, they left the table not with answers, but with a deeper understanding of the complexities and a commitment to continue exploring them.

About the Author

Aldo Grech's extraordinary journey, marked by a transition from a privileged upbringing in a conservative, right-leaning family to becoming a fervent advocate for empathy and a staunch critic of corporate manipulation, is the bedrock of his acclaimed book, "Silent Echoes." Born into a world where privilege and traditional values intermingled, Grech's narrative was initially shaped by the perspectives surrounding him. However, his extensive and diverse experience in the corporate realm, marked by an array of successes and failures across various cultures and industries, catalyzed a significant transformation in his worldview.

In "Silent Echoes," Grech harnesses this unique personal and professional evolution. He delves into the sophisticated and often covert realm of subliminal messaging and media influence, unearthing the intricacies of how some elites exploit these mechanisms to sway public opinion, often maneuvering the masses to act contrary to their own interests. This profound shift from being an insider of the status quo to a critical and insightful observer lends Grech an unparalleled authenticity. His insights transcend mere theory, being deeply rooted in a rich tapestry of real-life corporate experiences and a keen understanding of socio-political dynamics.

This metamorphosis instilled in Grech a profound empathy for the underprivileged, countering the narrative of his early years that often dismissed the unemployed and underemployed as 'lazy manipulators' and 'unworthy benevolence receivers'. His writings actively challenge these inherited narratives, shining a light on the manipulative tactics used to perpetuate such beliefs.

As a seasoned expert in transformative change within the business sector, Grech's career, which spans several continents, has seen him emerge as a trusted advisor to some of the world's leading corporations. His ability to connect innovative strategies with practical realities and his passion for continuous learning in diverse fields such as ethical leadership, organisational psychology and systems thinking have profoundly enriched his approach to change management.

In "Silent Echoes," Grech applies his deep-rooted expertise in transformational change and human psychology to dissect and critique the sophisticated strategies employed by the elite to manipulate public opinion. His book is a compelling exploration of how the principles governing organizational behaviour are often manipulated to craft narratives that promote the interests of a select few, often seeding conspiracy theories and shaping public discourse.

As an author, Grech's work is a synthesis of real-world examples, personal experiences, and theoretical insights, all woven together to unravel the complex web of psychological manipulation in media and other methods. His narrative is a powerful testament to the importance of personal growth and the need to continually challenge one's beliefs in the quest for truth and empathy.

Aldo Grech has redirected his expertise and passion towards what he terms "sustainable living," a concept that transcends the traditional understanding of environmental sustainability. For Grech, sustainable living embodies a holistic approach to life, encompassing not only ecological consciousness but also fostering psychological, spiritual, cultural, and community well-being. He perceives the current challenges in climate sustainability as a mirror reflecting our broader unsustainable lifestyles.

In his various talks and workshops, Grech emphasizes that true sustainability is about nurturing healthy lives, which in turn cultivates healthy families, vibrant cultures, and responsible companies. According to him, a life grounded in sustainability principles is the foundation for achieving genuine climate sustainability and global wealth and well-being. Grech views greed, with its tendency to exploit lives and resources for the last ounce of profit, as antithetical to his philosophy and sustainability of any kind. He articulates this as the pulverization of humanity for greed, a stark contrast to the nurturing, holistic approach to sustainable living.

Beyond the realm of writing, Grech is a respected speaker and coach, advocating for ethical leadership and authentic business practices. His commitment to unveiling the hidden tactics of manipulation reflects his broader dedication to social justice and ethical awareness. This blend of personal evolution, professional acumen, and a deep commitment to ethical integrity positions Aldo Grech as a vital voice in the current socio-political discourse, making him uniquely qualified to author "Silent Echoes," a book that delves into the profound impact of subliminal messaging and societal manipulation.

Sources

Unfair Game by Best Democracy -
https://www.youtube.com/watch?v=UJScbYEyapQ
The Great Hack by Karim Amer, Erin Barnett, Pedro Kos -
Netflix
The Social Dilemma by Davis Coombe, Vickie Curtis, Jeff
Orlowski - Netflix
Dark Money by Jane Mayer - Book
Devil's Bargain by Joshua Green
https://obr.uk/forecasts-in-depth/the-economy-forecast/brexit-
analysis/
https://www.ecb.europa.eu/pub/economic-bulletin/articles/202
3/html/ecb.ebart202303_01~3af23c5f5a.en.html
https://www.ons.gov.uk/businessindustryandtrade/business/bu
sinessservices/bulletins/businessinsightsandimpactontheukec
onomy/14december2023
https://www.thenation.com/article/archive/exclusive-behind-ko
ch-brothers-secret-billionaire-summit/
https://www.youtube.com/watch?v=th3KE_H27bs&t=319s
https://heartland.org/about-us/who-we-are/ivar-giaever/
https://www.gem.wiki/Richard_S._Lindzen#Fossil_Fuel_Intere
sts_Funding
https://insideclimatenews.org/news/02112020/john-christy-ala
bama-climate-contrarian/
https://www.desmog.com/sherwood-b-idso/
https://www.sourcewatch.org/index.php/S._Fred_Singer#Oil_I
ndustry_Contractor